BUFF LAMB
Lion of the Ozarks

RANDY H. GREER

Copyright © 2022 Randy Greer
All cover art copyright © 2022 Randy Greer
All Rights Reserved

This book is based on the real man Buff Lamb. No part of this book may be reproduced or transmitted in any form or by any means, electronic or mechanical, including photocopying, recording, or by any information storage and retrieval system, without permission in writing from the author.

Publishing Coordinator – Sharon Kizziah-Holmes

Paperback-Press
an imprint of A & S Publishing
Paperback Press, LLC

ISBN -13: 978-1-956806-61-8

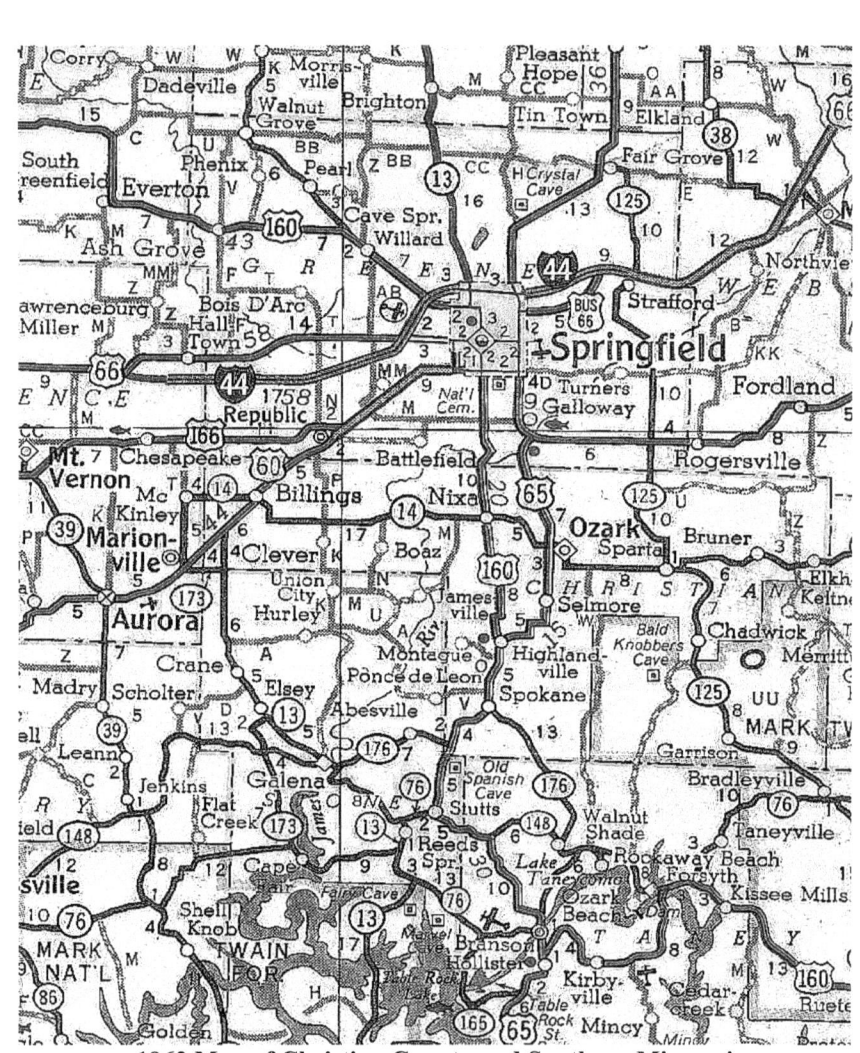

1962 Map of Christian County and Southern Missouri

Special Thanks To

Ray Speak an incredible wealth of information.
Paul Blue his remembrance of Buff and his brother Carter.
Corrine Duckworth Buff's ex-wife.
Penny Glossip Buff's daughter.
The Heatherly brothers; **Wandal, Russell and Gary.**
Dennis Beckett & Clady Beckett.

CONTENTS

Special Thanks To iv
Introduction..iii
Chapter One 1
   Cowboy to Daredevil 1
   The Nickname..4
   Adventure Beckons...5
Chapter Two 13
   Young Marshal 13
Chapter Three 20
   The Fighting Sheriff 20
   Looking for the Marshal… 26
Chapter Four 28
   The Sparta Wild Man..28
Chapter Five...36
   Murdered for No Reason 36
   Speaking of Wolves…..38
   Hell bound…..40
Chapter Six 43
   Speeding Days Are Over 43
Chapter Seven..49
   Run for Sheriff...49
   Headlines While Sheriff 53
Chapter Eight 54
   Go Back in Your House and Hide 54
Chapter Nine 58
   New Sheriff in Town 58
Chapter Ten 65
   Rockaway the Night 65
   Ambush…...69
   The Aftermath..71
Chapter Eleven...73
   Protecting Ozark 73
   Protect the Town…...73
Chapter Twelve 79
   Trouble in the Jail 79
Chapter Thirteen 86
   Murder, Threats and Suspicion..86

    Rumors Began to Fly… 88
    The Missing Woman Found… 90
    Buff is Going to Kill Me… 92
Chapter Fourteen 96
    The Rock Festival 96
Chapter Fifteen 103
    A Kinder, Gentler Lawman 103
Chapter Sixteen 110
    Lindenlure 110
Chapter Seventeen 115
    It's Time for the Sheriff To Go! 115
Chapter Eighteen 125
    Buff & Corrine 125
Chapter Nineteen 130
    I'll Win One Way or The Other 130
Chapter Twenty 137
    Last run for Sherriff 137
About the Author 147
People Interviewed for this Book 149
Sources 151

INTRODUCTION

This book is the story of one man's life. A man by happenstance that became a legend in his own time. These are the trials, tribulations, successes, mistakes, and marks that man made on Missouri for over 70 years.

To some, Buff Lamb was a savior, to others he was a tyrant and a bully. In writing this book, I have tried to reserve my judgments of Buff and present the facts contained in these pages as they were told to me. I hope you do the same.

Please consider that I have exposed someone's past and opened his life story for all the world to see. Something many of us would not want if given the choice.

Louard Buff Lamb was many things to many people. As you read this story you will find that when all the smoke clears, all the hurt feelings dissipate, just one man emerges from the storm; a man who stood tall and brave, the Lion of the Ozarks, Buff Lamb. Hate him, love him, or disregard him; the choice is now yours…

CHAPTER ONE

COWBOY TO DAREDEVIL

Floyd Ordway was cursing so loud it could be heard in the street and from the front of Buckner & Son Mercantile. Walking by at that time was Fredonia City Marshal A. B. "Arch" Mosely. The marshal heard the swearing and went inside to calm Ordway down. That proved to be a big mistake. One that would cost a man his life.

Ordway and Mosely did not like each other. Marshal Mosely had been forced to watch the Ordway home during an outbreak of smallpox. Ordway resented Mosely for drawing so much attention to his family during the outbreak. A large man, Ordway owned the Livery Stable in town where he often worked. Drunk and disorderly, Marshal Mosely asked him to step outside.

Once on the boardwalk, Mosely informed the big man that he was under arrest and would be escorting him to the jail across town. Ordway wasn't having any part of it. The two men wrestled. Inside Ordway's belt was a knife he carried to butcher hogs with. Ordway reached for the butcher knife, resting his large hand on it. "Leave me alone Arch, or I swear I will cut your throat and watch you bleed out!"

It began to rain while the two angry men faced each other in the street like two mad bulls refusing to give up any ground. Forty-three-year-old Mosely reached over and grabbed Ordway again and Ordway withdrew his knife from his belt. He was going stab the marshal.

Luckily, Mosely arched his back and reached inside his coat for his pistol. Without hesitation he fired three shots into the stomach of fifty-year-old Howsen "Floyd" Ordway. The big man fell backwards into the street. Dead. The marshal stepped closer to have a better look at Ordway. The pistol still smoking in his hand. Ordway died lying face up on the ground. Marshal Mosely would never forget the raindrops falling on the unblinking eyes of Floyd Ordway. It was an eerie sight.

Fearing for his life, Mosely walked ten miles in the rain to Princeton, where he gave himself up to Attorney J. T. Coleman. Folks were clannish in Caldwell County, and you never knew whose side they'd take in a shooting. Besides, Ordway had two sons that might want revenge.

Later that morning after shooting Ordway, Marshal Mosely went before the Princeton County Judge. After hearing the evidence, the court refused to press charges and released Mosely. The judge believed Marshal Mosely had acted in self-defense. Mosely had no choice but to defend himself against Ordway with the gun. The court may have seen it that way, but the Ordway family saw it as cold-blooded murder.

Four months after the shooting, William Lewis Lamb and Helena (Lena) Florence Martin married in Princeton. The Lambs were a prominent family in the area, having settled in Caldwell, County sometime around 1812.

William and Lena had been following the shooting in the newspaper. They may have even known the two men. But what happened next, surprised them both.

Two years passed and a blood feud had arisen between former Marshal Mosely and Floyd Ordway's son, Tom. In the south, kin folk are everything and it's reported that A.B. Mosely taunted Tom Ordway by informing him that he still had the gun he had killed his father with, and that if he had to, he'd shoot him, too! Tom Ordway was primed for a fight and eager to protect his family's good name.

One evening, the two met in the back of a saloon. An argument ensued. According to Tom Ordway, Mosely lunged at him with a knife, and Ordway shot and killed him. There were no witnesses. Just Ordway's word against a dead man. Was it poetic justice, or had the son of the man Moseley killed, placed the knife in Moseley's hand after he killed him? The jury found [1]Tom Ordway, not guilty, and that he had acted in self-defense.

Over the next nine years, Lena Lamb gave birth to three boys: Winfield Alexander, Hershel Thomas, and William Hoyt Lamb. Lena and William did their best to avoid the trouble that was brewing in Caldwell County.

In 1907, the Night Riders, a band of marauding vigilantes, shot a woman in the face and attempted to burn down her cabin. The woman survived the attack but was forced to flee to Indiana.

The Riders began as a peaceful citizens committee, but quickly transformed into a band of violent and destructive devils on horseback. These were the times the Lambs were living in.

In 1909, Tobacco Wars erupted in Caldwell County. It was the north growers against the southern growers. The Night Riders burned tobacco fields and a church. The folks who spoke out against the Night Riders called themselves the "Bob Cats".

The year 1912 proved a sad time for the Lambs. Lena, age 29, died of tuberculosis, leaving William with three boys to raise alone. William turned to family in Princeton to help with the children. But 3 years later, 1915, William was again married, this time to Flossie V. Brooks. Flossie was born in 1892 north of Caldwell, where she received a seventh-grade education.

Together, William and Flossie had six more boys and one daughter. Making the total number of children ten. Two of the boys died before the age of eleven.

One of the middle children, born in 1924, was Louard Elbert Lamb. That year, the Ku Klux Klan became very active in Kentucky and especially in Caldwell County. The community was split between those who supported the Klan, and those who didn't.

For the next several years, Klan violence and Prohibition tore across the country. There was no escaping it. The courthouse in Princeton KY was dynamited and over 200 citizens were arrested for crimes associated with illegal liquor and the Klan. The violence

---

[1] Tom Ordway later opened a Livery Stable. A few years after that, the Feds arrested him for running a moonshine still. Ordway died in 1938 at the age of 63.

continued in Kentucky until the National Guard restored peace and order. But before the government repealed prohibition, the "Great Depression" rained down upon the world.

During the hard times, the Lamb family struggled with crops and finances but managed to stay on their feet. The family worked hard to get through the lean times. There was always food on the table and the Lamb boys grew up quick and strong. But violence still lingered in Caldwell County like a haunting ghost.

The violence that pervaded the 1920's stayed with Caldwell County well into the 1930's. Louard was just eight years old when a mob stormed the county jail and tied up jailer [2]Curt Jones. The mob escaped with a prisoner, hanging him from a tree two miles outside of town. The prisoner was accused of dynamiting a store and injuring the owner. A few people believed the Ku Klux Klan was responsible for the murder but were afraid to say anything. Loose talk could get you killed, so the perpetrators went unpunished.

THE NICKNAME

Family and friends nicknamed Louard, "Buffalo" when he was a small boy, remembered Norman Ladd, a childhood friend of his. The name was given to him because he was tough and always charging forward like a buffalo. As he grew older, they shortened the nickname to "Buff". Everyone in Caldwell County who knew the youngster, referred to him as Buff Lamb. It was a nickname that would stay with the boy for the rest of his life.

William Lamb farmed and worked for the railroad for a short time. Clady, the youngest of the brood, remembered her father grew every crop imaginable. William was a good man and described as tall and thin, with gray eyes.

At age 13, fresh out of the 6th grade, Buff went to work on a Dude Ranch. City dwellers could spend a week riding horses, herding cattle, and enjoying the cowboy life. Buff took care of the livestock, remaining on the ranch for about a year.

---

[2] Two months after the mob incident, Jailer Curt Jones was back on duty. He was the jailer in October when 7 prisoners escaped from the jail by digging a hole in the wall.

At the age of 14, Buff then went to work for Harry Randolph. Randolph owned a restaurant in the Black Hawk community near Princeton. After learning how to cook, it wasn't long before Buff was managing the cafe. Buff continued to work for [3]Harry at the Twinkling Star Cafe throughout 1938 and 1939.

The year 1940 found Buff back at home with his parents and grandmother. Hattie Brooks, Flossie's 78-year-old mother, born in 1862, had come to live with the family in the early 1940s.

On the farm, the family planted and harvested tobacco and corn, and kept a few horses and livestock, but the farm life held no charm for young Buff Lamb.

ADVENTURE BECKONS

Clifford L. "Jack" Raum managed a Rodeo\Thrill show that traveled and performed throughout the Midwest. Raum began his career as a trick rider for Ringling Brothers' circus. During the years 1932 to 1937, Jack learned the circus business well enough to go out on his own, and most importantly, he knew how to sell himself.

Buff and his brothers had seen Raum's Circus. In those days it was every boy's dream to be a part of the excitement the circus offered. The boys were awed by Raum as he snapped a lit cigarette out of a patron's mouth with a bullwhip--at ten paces away!

[4]In 1941, at 17, Buff joined [5]Jack Raum's traveling Circus and Thrill attractions. Jack hired him as a rodeo performer to ride the bulls and bucking broncs. By July 1941, the show made its way to the state of Washington. The next month, they performed in

---

[3] According to Buff's nephew Dennis Beckett, Buff would remain friends with Harry for the rest of his life. When returning to Kentucky, Buff always tried to stop in to see "old Harry".

[4] Buff's sister Clady Beckett confirmed that Buff left home at 17, not 13 as many have said. Buff may have told people he left at 13 but he didn't. Clady passed away January 2022.

[5] Born June 7th, 1894, was a trick rider for Ringling Bro's Circus 1932-1937.

His stunt car drivers were known as Auto Maniacs and Red Devil Drivers.

Wilmington, Ohio.

The Circus traveled fast and hard, booking shows in small towns across the country. Lamb tried smoking and drinking, but more intoxicating than spirits served up at local taverns and saloons was the image he was building. He adorned himself with a cowboy hat and western chaps, even having a pair custom made with his name on them.

As the months passed, the teenager grew more confident of his size and strength. At night he slept in cattle trailers, the front seat of pickups, and haystacks under the stars, enduring all kinds of weather. It was a rare treat to check into a motel and enjoy a hot shower before falling exhausted onto a hard bed.

Like most young cowboys, he signed autographs and watched western movies at the local theaters. Buff also had his share of challenges from the locals. Buff soon found he was developing a way with the ladies and local boys didn't like the performers coming into town and flirting with their gals. Unlike local boys who ran with their friends, cowboys were loners, making them easy targets.

When challenged by local ruffians, Buff learned a valuable self-defense tactic. Hit first, hit fast, and hit hard! Getting the first lick in gave him a huge psychological advantage. If Buff could drop the guy in front of him, it sometimes took the "fight" out of the other challengers. It was a technique he would use for the next 40 years.

Tickets to the Fair cost 25 cents. For that quarter, you could watch trick riding, shooting, and the entire rodeo. Sometimes Daredevil acts were included. Those were the guys who got the girls. Girls liked the brave men who weren't afraid to face death.

In October, Buff was in Coshocton, Ohio, then Indiana, Kentucky, and all over the Midwest. But fame comes with a price and Buff was paying it.

According to Buff, he broke his legs 8 times and had his flesh ripped apart when a [6]bull gored him. Before leaving the hospital he received over 28 stitches in his leg. He was lucky to have survived. Buff would later say he had broken almost every bone in his body. If that is true, Buff spent a lot of time bandaged and in a cast.

So, Buff changed careers. He became a stuntman and daredevil.

---

[6] Confirmed by an ex-wife.

He traded wild animals for machines. Now he recklessly drove automobiles and motorcycles. For the next year, Buff crashed and flipped cars. He jumped motorcycles over trucks and through flaming hoops of fire. Buff bragged that he was not afraid of "*anything*"! He learned something important about himself—he craved attention and excitement. And then came the war with the Germans and Japanese.

On December 7th, 1941, the Japanese attacked Pearl Harbor, and the nation went into a panic. Several of the cowboys raced to their local recruiting station to get in on the fight. Buff was one of them.

Buff was the second of his brothers to register for the draft. Registering on June 30, 1942. He was living in Dulaney, an unincorporated town. Broken bones and injuries kept Buff out of the Army. Brother Virgil joined before him, in February 1942. Older brother James Carter, registered on September 23, 1942.

By the mid-1940s, the Kentucky Cowboy was on the road and feeling invincible. How? I don't know. By now, his leg had been shattered 8 times. Bulls had gored him several times, and Buff's jawbone had been segmented together. Not to mention, his muscles were strained and twisted.

Before his 21st birthday, Buff had [7]suffered concussions, contusions, broken bones, and several surgeries, in the name of proving how tough he was. He suffered more injuries than nearly all of his fellow performers. Buff was no stranger to pain, he lived it every day.

In 1945, Buff was as tough as knots on an oak tree. He was six feet tall, with brown eyes, muscled arms, and ready for adventure. He was not afraid of anyone or anything. In his eyes, he had tamed man, beast, and machine.

Brothers Virgil and Carter returned home from the War and Buff was eager to see them and welcome them home. [8]Buff's family was a big part of his life and always would be.

In between working on the Miller 101 Ranch outside of Detroit, and driving a truck, Buff met 24-year-old Jean E. Ray, a nurse from Wayne County. A short time later the two were dating. Jean

---

[7] Buff Lamb was the Evel Knievel of the 1940s. But his cars and bikes were not tricked out and safety proofed.
[8] Unless it came to the woman he was with.

was enamored with the tall, handsome cowboy from Kentucky. Buff was all man, and his shy manners put the young nurse under his spell.

Justice Leo O. Nye married the two on the Miller Ranch in Michigan, on March 11, 1945. Buff and Jean were dressed in western garb on horseback. Buff bore the image of a western cowboy, and he was exactly that, a cowboy.

They moved in with Jean's parents who lived on Hubbard Street in Detroit, Michigan. Buff was twenty-one but felt twice his age. He limped a lot and often had headaches he chose to ignore. By all standards it was a miracle he could walk at all.

One month later, showman Jack Raum married Bebe Cooper. The two bought the Elias Bedford Russell Farm (162 acres) about two and a half miles west of Ozark, Missouri.

Elias was born in Christian County in 1876 and had owned the farm for over 40 years. But Elias was 69 and turning his attention to running a store in Ozark. A few weeks passed when Jack visited Buff.

"Buff, I've bought this ranch down in Ozark, Missouri, and you're the man to run it for me.

"Really? How many acres?"

"162 and I'm planning on running a few steers and horses on it".

"Where the hell is Ozark?"

"It's south of Springfield, near the Arkansas border. It is beautiful down there. A river runs through the town, and it has a huge Courthouse on the square. I was hoping you and Jeannie would take care of it for me...until Bebe and I can get settled down there!"

It was a chance of a lifetime. Buff could spend more time with Jean and do what he liked best—running cattle and managing a ranch. Besides, the pain from his injuries was taunting him day and night. But how would Jean respond?

Jean had reservations about leaving Detroit. What would she do in a small town on the edge of the Ozark Mountains? Jean's father John was not happy about the move either.

Young Buff

Stunt Driver Buff Elbert Lamb with broken leg

Buff on motorcyle

Friend with Buff

Buff's Draft Card

"She's a city girl, Buff, she won't like it down there with the moonshiners and mountain lions! Didn't they hang some vigilantes on the square down there?"

"Yes, sir, but that was a long time ago, and it's pretty peaceful now!"

A long time ago? It was sixty years ago. The Bald Knobbers had clothed themselves in devil masks and rode the Ozark hills. Under the cloak of darkness, they sought anyone who opposed them. During those turbulent years, citizens were run out of the county, and in severe cases, tied to a tree and severely whipped.

Things came to a head on the night of March 11, 1887. Sixteen-year-old Billy Walker and his men broke into a cabin and killed some people inside. During the melee, Billy Walker was wounded.

Billy Walker was hung on the Ozark town square, along with his father and a couple of other Bald Knobbers. Tragically, Billy had to be hung twice because the first time the rope was too long and prevented Billy's neck from breaking. They carried him back up on the platform, and the trapdoor was once again dropped. The hanging in Ozark marked the end of the Christian County Bald

Knobbers.

Elias Bedford Russell, the man Jack Raum bought the ranch from, would have been 13 years old when the hanging took place. If Elias did not see the hanging as a boy, which he most definitely could have, he heard about it the next day. In those days, people came from all over the country to see a hanging.

Eventually, the Bald Knobbers disbanded, but not before leaving a trail of shootings, hangings, and violence behind them. Many of the relatives still lived in Ozark, but their feud had nothing to do with new folks moving into the county. The question on Buff's mind was, "Would Jean like the Ozarks?"

CHAPTER TWO

YOUNG MARSHAL

Summer of 1945: Franklin D. Roosevelt had died and Harry S. Truman from Missouri, was President. World War II was winding down as Buff and Jean moved to the Ozark ranch. They quickly attempted to build a life for themselves. The couple made friends and received an invitation to Thanksgiving dinner at Mrs. Grace Smith's house later that year.

In 1911, Ms. Grace Haguewood married H. C. Smith. Her husband had been a blacksmith in town. It was an honor to be invited to the Smith home.

Also attending the dinner was Holland Blevins and possibly his sister. He was the son-in-law of Mrs. Smith. and the brother of a young girl named Mary Lee Blevins. Mary Lee had caught Buff's wistful eye the moment he arrived in Ozark. She was tall, thin, and beautiful. The kind of woman Buff was attracted to. But for now, the cowboy kept that to himself.

Occasionally, the couple went to the picture show in Ozark. On November 29, 1945, they watched "Sheriff of Cimarron", with Sunset Carson and Linda Stirling. Unlike Detroit, there were no tall buildings, popular stores, or restaurants to dine in. Jean felt like she had traveled back in time a hundred years. Compared to Detroit, Ozark was a roadside stop along the highway. The town had nothing to offer.

The remoteness of Ozark drove Jean crazy. She had never experienced country life. The culture shock made her realize she had to get back to the big city. Jean's father had been right, she was a city girl through and through.

The couple argued and Buff spent as much time as he could away from his new bride working. He took a job as a mechanic in Springfield on Campbell Street. He did odd jobs, like digging graves by hand and building fences. But the marriage still suffered. It became apparent to the couple the single reason they married was a case of infatuation.

The excitement had worn off. Jean was no longer in love with Buff. He was as country as the people around him. Then, she heard that Buff was caught flirting with a Blevins girl in town. Jean moved back to Michigan and filed for divorce. The divorce became final on November 7, 1946. The couple had been married just over a year. Maybe Buff wasn't cut out for the married life.

Buff remained in Ozark. It was his new home. Brother [9]Carter had moved there as well. Something unexplainable kept the cowboy in the small town. It turned out to be a good move because through a twist of fate, the Kentucky cowboy was about to get noticed.

The ink hadn't dried on the divorce papers when, a month later, Buff was seeing Holland's [10]twenty-year-old sister [11]Mary Lee Blevins. Mary Lee was the daughter of [12]Claude and Lennie Blevins. She had five brothers and two sisters. The young beauty loved the cowboy and knew from the beginning she wanted to marry him.

The two dated for a short time, and before long, Mary Lee was pregnant. The two married in Arkansas three months later, on March 1st, 1947. Buff was 23 years old, and this was his second marriage. Buff used the name "Lonard" instead of "Louard". He had been divorced for 113 days and for at least 90 of those days, he

---

[9] Carter eventually worked at Anheuser-Busch in Springfield, Missouri. Busch opened in Springfield in 1966.
[10] Mary Lee was born May 16, 1926.
[11] Mary Lee Blevins had been a softball champion in Ozark High School.
[12] Claude Blevins had been a wolf hunter in 1930-1940. He had killed over 20 wolves. The price for the hides was between 10-20 dollars.

had been seeing Mary Lee.

The couple rented a house in Ozark and seemed to do well. When the County Fair came to town, Buff was a clown in the rodeo. Pregnant wife Mary Lee cheered him on from the fairground stands. In those days, Buff would spin around in town in his army jeep and wave at everyone. Especially the young girls. Many of them waved back.

When Buff walked into a café, people took notice of the young, handsome cowboy. He was tall, friendly, outgoing, and respected by the townsfolk. Then, as it would many times in the future, Buff's life took a turn. Here are the two most common folk tales of what happened. Keep in mind, I call them folk tales. Stories handed down through the years.

The story goes, Buff drove into town one day and entered a café on the square. While inside, two rock growers from Chadwick walked in and sat down beside the young cowboy. Their plan was to badger him.

The former stuntman turned cowhand invited the two to step outside. Sonny, the larger of the two, spoke first.

"Now what are you…"

Buff struck hard and quick, like an Ozark Mountain Copperhead snake! It was a technique Buff had learned in the back pens of rodeos and small towns across the Midwest. Attack first and attack hard. The first blow is always the most important.

Buff knocked Sonny backward off the sidewalk into the street. The blow put Sonny flat on his back. The smaller man ran to his aide. Backing away from the ranch hand, the two dislodged a stream of expletives and limped across the square to Ford's Pool Room.

Staying around would mean getting the stuffing knocked out of them. Buff walked back inside the café and paid for his meal. The story of what had happened reached everyone's ears by sundown that day.

Another story has Buff going into a bar and ordering a glass of milk. When the bartender snickered and refused the Kentuckian, Buff walked over to Ford's Pool Hall.

"How much for a pool stick? I want to buy one."

"That'll be .20 cents."

Buff bought the stick, walked outside, and broke the cue over his knee. He threw away the smaller half and entered the saloon with the larger, jagged half. Buff walked up to the bartender and slammed the sharp stick on the bar, "I'll take that milk now!" The bartender quickly obliged. The barroom patrons could not wait to get home and tell what they just witnessed.

Whatever he did that day, Buff got the attention of Sheriff [13]Lige Reed and [14]Marshal Ross Robertson. So, when a night Marshal's job came open, the town thought of Buff Lamb. The 23-year-old accepted the position at a rate of $5 a week.

Just twenty-three and a town Marshal. It made the young cowboy feel important, like a big man in the small town. Someone that held respect. Buff worked as a City Marshal at night and during the day he continued to do odd jobs in the county.

After the sheriff went home, the new Marshal pinned on his badge and was ready to catch the bad guys. In a town of a few hundred, there weren't that many arrests to be made, especially after six in the evening. The whistle-stop burg became a ghost town after five, but that didn't stop the marshal from looking for bad guys. He had a gun on his hip, a badge on his shirt, and the confidence to destroy any obstacle in front of him. The criminal element in Ozark had better watch out!

September 1947, Buff's only son Randall Ray (Roho) Lamb was born. Buff and Mary Lee could not have been prouder parents.

The newborn baby in the house created a new problem. Buff was not getting the attention he wanted at home. He threw himself into his work, as he often did. He began to talk about going back on the rodeo circuit. The couple fought and Mary Lee left Buff.

Louard Elbert (Buff) Lamb and Mary Lee divorced in May 1948. The marriage had lasted little more than a year. Just like his first relationship. Only this time he left behind a seven-month-old baby.

Buff took a break from marshaling and went back on the road as a bull and bronc-riding cowboy. Mary Lee relied on the kindness

---

[13] Sheriff Lige Reed had been the undersheriff of Newt Maples and Clay Hodges. They elected Lige sheriff in 1944. Clay Hodges would have been the Sheriff but the law at that time prevented a Sheriff from succeeding himself in office.

[14] Marshal Robertson had started as a guard at the Missouri State Penitentiary in Jefferson City in 1933. By 1938 he was Ozark's Night Marshal. He has also owned the Appetite Café on the Northside of the square.

of friends and family to help raise their son. Buff was out of their lives.

The roving buckaroo returned to Ozark in the fall of that year and decided he could not live without Mary Lee. He missed her and wanted her back. Mary Lee was hesitant at first, but finally gave in to the cowboy's charm. The two remarried in November 1948. Buff used the first name of "Lavard" instead of "Louard". Their divorce had lasted less than six months.

Everything seemed fine until history repeated itself. Mary Lee became pregnant, and that changed everything. With one baby at home and another on the way, Buff quit his marshal job and headed out on the road, leaving Ozark in the summer of 1949.

It was the proverbial straw that broke the camel's back. Buff was a selfish, self-centered, self-serving man who thought only of himself. [15]Mary Lee divorced Buff and moved to Kansas. Buff's daughter [16]Penny was born in Wichita. Her father was unaccounted for. Buff returned to Christian County in 1950. He had never seen his baby daughter and wouldn't for a long time.

In June of that year, Buff was a Daredevil driver with the "Hell on Wheels Thrill Show". Buff excited audiences in Ava, Missouri, when he rolled a car over from end to end. Buff was a celebrity in Christian and Douglas County.

A few weeks later, with his hat in his hand, Buff met with the city council and secured his marshal job back. They were happy to have the cowboy return to their town. Like always, Buff used his position to meet young women. Buff could not leave the girls alone.

[17]Paul Blue, one of Buff's and Carter's good friends,

---

[15] Mary Lee would re-marry in 1955 and work as a newspaper editor. When Mary Lee became ill, she resigned from the position, and at the young age of 42, Mary Lee passed away at her home.

[16] Pamela Penny Glossip reported that "Mom had no idea where Buff was when I was born." The night before Penny was born, October 9, 1949, back in Ozark, someone dynamited the newspaper office. Thirty windows were blown out of the building. No one was hurt.

[17] Paul liked Buff's brother Carter better. He was easier to get along with. Paul and Bernice eventually married.

remembered the night Buff pulled his girlfriend over.

"I had been on a date with Bernice in her car. Later that evening, Bernice dropped me off at my milk truck I had parked in an alley. I had seen Buff earlier on the town square. I used to race my motorcycle against his car on slow nights. For some reason, after Bernice dropped me off, I decided to go by her house."

"When I got to the bridge, Buff had Bernice pulled over. I knew what he was doing. He was pulling Bernice over to see who she was. I grabbed a pipe I used to open ornery milk can lids with and marched up to him. I thought Buff might want to fight. Buff apologized and said he did not know Bernice was my girl. Buff let her go, and I got back in my truck and left."

"The next day I saw Buff, and he waved me over. I thought he might want to fight after the way I had talked to him the night before. Buff was like that. He did not take anything from anyone! Instead, he apologized again and after that, he tipped his hat to Bernice every time he saw her."

Returning from the road this time and getting his old job back, Buff decided he was ready to settle down. He could not help who he was, but he was not going back on the road again or leaving Christian County.

As for Mary Lee, she returned to Ozark, hating Buff for the way he had treated her and their children. Buff found out how much she despised him when he stopped her for a minor traffic violation. Ray Speak remembered the incident.

"Clay called me to the sheriff's office and said, "Rufus, come up here and look at Guff's head! He's got a bruise on it." Buff had stopped Mary Lee down by the pottery shop and she beat the crap out of him with her high-heel shoe!" Ray Speak still laughs about it.

For the next year, Buff kept a low profile and his nose to the grindstone. And he stayed away from Mary Lee. Buff was aggressive and did his job better than his predecessors. He and Sheriff Clay Greer Hodges often worked together. The two were good friends and Clay helped mentor Buff in those early years.

So, when Buff heard that Sheriff Hodges had been attacked by some prisoners, he rushed to see his friend at home. How dare anyone attack his friend and a man he admired! He would sort this out and damn quick!

Marshal Buff Lamb

Marshal Lamb (Center). Sheriff Clay Hodges on Buff's right.

CHAPTER THREE

THE FIGHTING SHERIFF

Two weeks before Clay was assaulted, Buff walked into the Sheriff's office as summoned. Compared to Buff; Clay Hodges looked more like a business manager than a county sheriff. With his fedora hat and white shirt, he looked more like a politician, insurance salesman, or City Mayor. Clay's badge was pinned on his shirt and his .38 pistol on his hip under his jacket. He was friendly, honest, brave, and respected by everyone in Christian County.

Buff looked more like a western cowboy. A little like Gary Cooper in the 1940 movie "The Westerner".

"Morning!"

"Hello, Guff. Quiet night?"

"Yeah, except for Mrs. Gold's dog barking all night. I swear the cats in this town taunt that dog." Clay stepped from behind his desk.

"[18]Guff, for the past year, I've watched you and I like the way you handle yourself. You've proven yourself to me in this town. You're finally taking this job seriously."

"Well, since me and Mary Lee...."

"I know. I hated to hear about you two. Guff, I called you up here because I'm giving you a County Commission. Ben Hart and I

---

[18] Clay referred to Buff as "Guff". Buff called Sheriff Clay Hodges "Teebob" said Ray Speak.

can't be everywhere at night, so I want you to take this commission. From now on, you have my authority to answer calls and make arrests anywhere in the county. If you arrest someone outside the city, come and get me and I'll lock 'em up."

"Thanks, Teebob!"

"I guess you heard, Marshal Coots over in Webster County shot and killed a man?"

"Yep."

"The point is this job is dangerous and none of us are bulletproofed. Not even you!"

"I know, thanks Teebob. By the way, any trouble with those three that robbed the café?"

Buff was talking about George S. Harwell (20), Patrick McPhee (20), and Tommie O. Young (22). On August 22nd, 1951, the three broke into the Nixa café and Thelma's café. The three got away with some jukebox nickels, pennies, and $14 cash. Sheriff Clay Hodges and Deputy Ben Hart arrested and placed the trio in the Christian County jail.

Seven days later, Ronald Wyrick (18) and Alfred Hoffman (20) stole a car from R.W. Fugett in Ozark. A Highway Patrolman captured the two Air Force deserters west of St. Louis, Missouri.

They took the two back to Ozark and placed them in the jail on the third floor with Harwell, McPhee, and Young. The five were all about the same age and no doubt bragged about their criminal escapades.

For the next two weeks, sitting in jail together, the five boys hatched a plan. They would knock out the old Sheriff, grab his keys and escape from custody. They planned the escape for September 12th, 1951, during the evening meal. The others would distract the sheriff, while Wyrick would be the one to take him out.

"No Guff, they're fine, but those two Air Force deserters seem a little cocky. Especially the one they call Donald Wyrick. Something ain't right about that boy. He has a mean streak in him. He's up to something."

"I can talk to him. He'll tell me what he's up to or I'll pin his ears back!"

"No, there's no need for that. Besides, I'm taking him and Hoffman to the Penitentiary in a few days. They'll get a new kind of education up there!"

"Well, I have to get home. I need some sleep before my shift tonight."

Walking across the courthouse lawn, Buff heard tires squealing on the west side of the square. Glancing around the courthouse, he observed several boys hollering, "Willie Peel! Willie Peel!"

Which meant for the youngster in the 1937 Ford to burn rubber on the street. The youth complied. He revved up his engine and slammed it into gear! Too bad he didn't see the city marshal watching him.

"What's your name, boy?"

"Raymond Speak sir."

"Got a hot-rod here, don't ya boy?"

"It's okay."

"Well, today it earned you a $5 ticket. I'd better never catch you up here squealing those tires again. If I do, I'll take you and your car off the square!"

"Yes, sir."

The city marshal walked away, admiring the youth's spunk and his car. He thought to himself; that boy has a future if he can stay out of trouble. Teenager Ray Speak was thinking; that old goose caught me this time, but he won't the next!

Two days later, Sheriff Hodges reported for work at the courthouse. He passed John Dean Harris, the coroner, on the bottom floor and waved to him. On the second floor, he passed county prosecuting attorney, Bill Davenport.

"Sheriff, I need to speak to you about Buff! He..."

"I don't have time for it now, Bill. Whatever Buff did, tell me about it later. I have to get upstairs and feed my prisoners."

The prosecutor was trying to head off another one of Marshal Lamb's fiascos. The night before, Buff had damaged a man's car. After stopping a prominent citizen's son, the boy developed an attitude. In retaliation, Buff tore his car (a new convertible) apart.

When the boy's dad heard about it and saw his new convertible, he was livid! Had Buff lost his mind? Why would he rip a car apart like that? Did he know whose car it was? The man demanded the city pay for repairs, and that they prosecute Buff.

"Buff was always doing stuff like that! They wuz always making complaints about him. Clay would get so mad at Buff! But they wuz friends." Said a former Lamb associate.

Back upstairs in the courthouse, Clay retrieved the lockup keys from his desk drawer. He retrieved his pistol and exchanged it for a thumper (small head-knocker). It was time to give the lockups some coffee.

As Clay walked down the cell block, he tapped his keys on the bars. "Wyrick! Hoffman! I'm taking you boys to the pen in the morning. I want to get an early start to Jefferson City."

"I don't know if we're going, Sheriff. We've gotten used to you and your deputy!" said Wyrick. Hoffman, Patrick McPhee, George Harwell, and Tommie Young all laughed. They looked to Wyrick as their leader. He was taller than the rest and still dressed in his khaki uniform. He appeared to be the smartest of the gang.

"Oh, you and Hoffman are going! I'll be in to get you around six."

"Whatever you say, Sheriff." Hoffman flipped a lit cigarette against the wall. Sparks flew everywhere. Hoffman, dressed in a blue jean shirt and pants, wasn't too smart but he'd jump in a fight if given the chance.

After herding the boys back into their cells, Clay walked into his office where he met Deputy Ben Hart. Deputy Hart was an older man, clean-shaven, with glasses, and well dressed like Clay.

"Something's not right with those boys, Ben. You'd better be careful when you feed them at noon."

"What do you suppose they're up to Sheriff?"

"I'm not sure, but that Wyrick kid may try something. Keep an eye on him."

"I'll watch them, boss."

That evening, Clay opened his desk drawer and disarmed himself. He started to walk away when something told him to keep the pistol. Listening to the voice, Clay closed the drawer and took the pistol with him to feed the prisoners. Something he had never done before. It was a last-second decision that would save his life.

"Let's go boys, time to head back to the tank!" Sheriff Hodges hadn't noticed 18-year-old Ronald Wyrick hiding behind a solid door, waiting to ambush him.

As Hodges herded the men into the large room, Wyrick jumped from behind the door. Next, with all his strength, he struck the sheriff in the back of the head with a heavy cigarette lighter he had placed in a sock.

"Whack!" The homemade club found its mark on the sheriff's skull. He stumbled, and nearly blacked out. His knees buckled, and for a second, the room went black. The blow should have killed him.

Faltering awkwardly to his right, the aging lawman reverted to survival mode. Blood soaked his head and shirt. His mind went blank, but his body kept moving. Dying wasn't an option. Not today. Not at the hands of these five punks!

But the attack did not end there. Wyrick swung and struck the sheriff two more times. The sheriff's face and neck were bright red with blood. How was he on his feet? He should be dead on the floor!

"I turned and grabbed him with my left hand. Pulled my gun out and hit him with the flat side of it, knocking him out and through the door," Sheriff Clay Hodges stated after the attack. Sheriff Hodges continued to stand his ground. With Wyrick laying on the floor, unconscious, Alfred Hoffman (20), strongest of the five assailants, rushed the sheriff who now appeared weakened from his encounter with Wyrick. Hoffman saw this as his opportunity to finish the job and make a run for it.

Somehow, the farm-boy turned sheriff, pivoted, and slugged his next assailant. The blow knocked Hoffman backward into a wall. That's when Deputy Ben Hart heard the commotion and rushed into the fray.

Hart pulled his gun on the prisoners and aimed it at their chests. He would shoot every damn one of them if they didn't back off the Sheriff. When Clay saw Hart, he shouted, "Don't shoot!" The deputy came to his senses in the nick of time and lowered his revolver.

"Pick up your friends and drag them into those cells! And if I hear any more, from any of you, I'll…"

"Help me out of here, Ben." Clay did not want the prisoners to see him if he passed out. Sheriff Hodges saw a doctor who bandaged his head. The large cuts required stitches. Wyrick and Hoffman saw a doctor as well. Wyrick's head injury only needed a bandage. If not for deputy Hart that day, the boys would have killed Clay. Marshal Lamb was one of the first to hear of Clay's incursion.

"Those sons of...."

"Now Buff, we're all pissed about those thugs, but Clay says not to touch them."

"I don't care, Ben. If you give me the keys, I'll teach them frog skinners a lesson they'll never forget. Especially that Wyrick punk!"

"Let's see what Clay wants to do first."

Ben was the voice of reason. He was older than Buff and much more reasonable. That's why Clay picked him for the job. If he had let Buff off the leash, he would have beaten them within an inch of their lives. Buff respected and admired Clay Hodges. They were more than just fellow lawmen; they were friends.

Sheriff Hodges returned to work the next afternoon. Wyrick and Hoffman received twelve years each at the Missouri State Penitentiary. The charge was felonious assault and attempted escape. The other prisoners received three-year sentences.

If Wyrick had not tried to escape and only committed the assault, he might have served two or three years. In the words of movie star John Wayne, "Life is hard, but it's harder when you're stupid."

In 1952, Wyrick appealed his case, stating that the assault on Hodges was not premeditated. The average sentence for a non-planned assault was five years. Wyrick's appeal went before the court. They turned it down. Wyrick would have to finish his sentence.

While incarcerated, [19]Ronald Wyrick always sent Clay a Christmas card. In return, Clay sent him one back. The two continued their correspondence until they released Wyrick from prison. After that, Wyrick disappeared.

By spring 1952, the Ozark marshal was in love again, or so he thought. On April 25th, 1952, Louard Elbert Lamb married Ruby Jo (Jo) White in Harrison, Arkansas. [20]Ruby Jo had enlisted in the

---

[19] A Ronald T Wyrick died in 1994. This may be the same Wyrick.
[20] Ruby Jo was discharged in 1943.

Army during World War II and served five months as a WACC.

Ruby Jo differed from Buff's other two wives. Ruby Jo kept a tight leash on the handsome, badge-wearing lawman. One former resident remembered the time he saw Ruby Jo smack Buff in public. "Jo didn't take any crap off Buff!" recalled Buff's friend. As for Buff, it was the fourth time he had vowed to love, honor, and obey a woman, but it was far from the last. He was just warming up.

The Marshal was out there almost every night looking for burglars and safecrackers. Yet, unbeknownst to Buff, in February 1954, it was "he" who was under surveillance.

LOOKING FOR THE MARSHAL...

It was a Wednesday morning around 3:00 am and the [21]Jackson brothers were locked up in the jail. Stewart couldn't sleep and stood staring out his cell window from the third floor.

"Get up Sonny and look at this!"

"Leave me alone, Stewart, I'm trying to sleep!"

"No! You gotta see this! Someone is following the Marshal around town!"

Sonny rose from his bunk, and sure enough, a little blue car was following the night marshal while he made his rounds. It was Buff's normal routine to head home around three in the morning when his shift ended.

"Look! Look! They're coming back, Sonny! Damn! They is robbing the Farmer's Exchange! You reckon they wuz in the Army? Maybe they wuz recon?"

Six hours later, around 9:00 am, Sheriff Hodges learned that the Farmer's Exchange had been robbed of $886.69. Clay called Buff in when he learned the Jackson brothers had witnessed the crime.

It infuriated Buff when he heard what had happened. It was a tremendous blow to his ego. No one bested Marshal Buff Lamb! No one! The two investigated the theft but came up empty-handed, and the case went cold.

In May 1954, Buff took a leave of absence from his job. His

---

[21] Not real names, but an accurate description of what happened.

father, William Lewis Lamb, had died of cerebral arteriosclerosis. His arteries had hardened in his brain. William Lamb was 76 years old.

Back from Kentucky, Buff was on night patrol on June 21st, around 2:30 am, when he heard a noise down the street by the Farmer's Exchange. The night marshal raced to the back of the building, wondering if it were the same burglars from last February?

He was right, but he was too late. The burglars had seen him coming and bolted from the scene, leaving their tools behind. It'd be the last time they'd try safe cracking in Ozark. Marshal Lamb was onto them.

Deputy Ben Hart with the young men who attacked Sheriff Hodges.

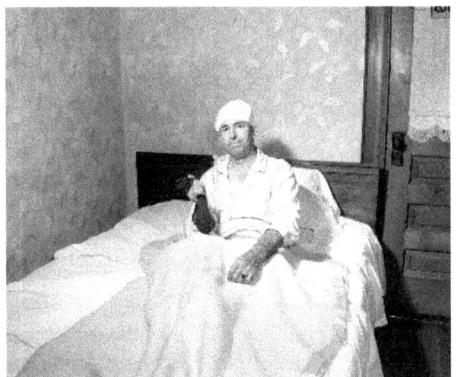
Clay Hodges after attack

CHAPTER FOUR

THE SPARTA WILD MAN

The job was getting to Buff. All jobs do, eventually. Maybe it was his father's death, home life, or maybe he was missing his children? He refused to acknowledge Roho and Penny were his offspring, but he knew one hundred percent they were. Nonetheless, Buff felt more and more frustrated. He hardly slept, which caused him to be full of anger and anxiety. [22]Jimmy Dalton recalled the night he rode with Buff in his patrol car. Jimmy was 17 years old. In those days, kids rode in the patrol car with Buff to keep him company. It was not an uncommon practice. Lots of law enforcement officers did the same thing, and still do.

"Suddenly Buff stopped the car, got out, and walked over to Rex Workman, who he had stopped. Workman tried to get out of the car but didn't do it fast enough, so Buff jerked him out of the car and started kicking him! He kicked [23]Workman so hard he fell on his back. To my knowledge, the man hadn't done a thing! Buff got back in the car and we left. Buff never said a word about why

---

[22] Name withheld, although permitted to use by the witness.
[23] Rex Workman died on March 26th, six years later. A drunken driver killed him. As for Buff, in the words of at least one person who knew him well; "He could be mean, real mean!"

he had stopped the man or kicked him to the ground."

November 1954, Buff was searching for 12-year-old Joan Rantz who had come up missing from her bus stop in Highlandville, Missouri. The little girl had gotten off the school bus to walk home when she dropped her books. That is when two men grabbed her, put a hood over her face, and tied her hands.

For the next 18 hours, everyone in the county searched for the missing girl and feared for their own child's safety.

After trying to decide what to do with the girl, the men dropped her back off at her bus stop. According to the young girl, the men rarely spoke, and she could not identify them. To this writer's knowledge, they never captured the kidnappers.

Throughout his career, Marshal Lamb bragged to friends that he was "fearless".

"Nothing scares me. I've ridden bulls, broncs, flipped cars and crashed motorcycles. I'm not afraid of man nor beast!" touted the tall, muscular night watchman. But he was wrong. The Marshal could be frightened, and it all happened on a dark and moonless night in Ozark.

*

In Klamath Falls, Oregon, Edith Mae "Tillie" Spoon, and her husband, had been fighting and arguing for weeks. One day when her husband Glen was out, she packed her things and left the home. Several days later, Edith had not returned, so Glen filed for divorce.

With no physical address to send the divorce papers to, Glen placed an ad in the paper, stating if he didn't hear from Edith soon, the divorce would become final in December 1954.

The ad ran once a week in the newspaper. The last one ran on November 10th and there would be no more. Edith Mae had hit rock bottom in her life, and she knew she could not go back to Glen. Not now, not when everyone knew Glen was divorcing her, allegedly for "cruel and inhumane treatment." Enter forty-two-year-old Aaron V. Dean and his thirty-four-year-old partner, James Douglas Meek.

The two men met Edith in a saloon. That night, they decided they would drive Edith southeast across the country. Along the way, the three sang and drank while they crossed state line after state line.

Patrolling Ozark in November 1954, around 3:00 am, Buff observed a car driving behind storefronts. The vehicle was edging slowly through alleys. At that time of the morning, one might see one or two cars before daylight, but you knew who they were. The men in this car weren't from Christian County and seemed very suspicious. The wary vehicle slowed even more, then circled behind the MFA Exchange. Buff was sure he was about to catch some safecrackers.

While the town slept warmly in their beds, Buff got out of his patrol car and crept behind a smoldering trash can. He watched a possum scurry across the street and onto the courthouse lawn. Buff was a hunter stalking his prey.

A few yards away, two men exited a car and seemed very confused as they walked around to the rear of the building. Buff ran across Delmar Clinton's backyard and moved in on the suspects' vehicle. That's when he heard voices.

"I dunno Aaron, it might work."

"All I know is, we have to get this done and get the hell out of here!"

"Stop right there, boys!"

The two men froze like deer caught in headlights. The burly lawman shined his flashlight in the stranger's faces.

"What are you boys doing here?" The men looked at one another for an answer and then back at Buff.

"We're uh...looking for...you see we have this uh, friend and..."

"Are you boys safecrackers? What're your names?"

"No sir, we're not robbing anyone. My name is Aaron Dean, and this here is my friend James Meek. We've driven here from Oregon, and we were, uh...well it's like this deputy, we uh..."

"Quit chewing on it and spit it out! What are you two frog skinners up to? Never mind! Stand there where I can see you and don't move. If you run, they'll be singing hymns over your bodies."

The thirty-one-year-old marshal searched the front seat of the car and glove box but found nothing. Then in the back seat, he found someone covered up with a blanket.

"Hey, you! Wake up!" The body under the blanket didn't move. "Damn you, I said *wake up!*" Buff poked the body with his flashlight and a woman's arm fell out from underneath the blanket.

Buff jerked back the cover and shined the light on the woman's face. "Damn you, I said...*Gawd almighty*!" Buff jerked backward, knocking his hat off. He couldn't get out of the car fast enough!

After pulling back the blanket, Buff had revealed a woman's face and upper torso. The woman's eyes and mouth were wide open, and her eyes fixated. A blind man in a dark cave could see the woman was dead! Buff had reacted as if he had opened a sack full of copperhead snakes.

"*Son-of-a-bitch! Who the Hell is that? What are you boys doing with a dead woman in your back seat?*"

"Well, you see deputy, we were uh, uh, you know we were uh...". The two men edged their way toward the marshal. Maybe they could jump the deputy and make a quick getaway? The marshal was big, but one of them was carrying a knife.

"Stop right there! You boys take another step and I'll drop you where you stand!"

Buff withdrew his revolver so fast it would have made Wyatt Earp proud. Then again, fear sharpens a man's reflexes. Buff pointed his six-gun waist high at the two. From this range, he could gut shoot them both. He had caught two murderers attempting to hide a body in town. His pistol shook from nervousness. Coming face to face with the dead woman, and then the men attempting to rush him, had taken a toll on his nerves.

"Take these cuffs and snap them on! You boys are going to jail! Any weapons on you?" One man spoke up, "I have a switchblade."

"I'll take that!" Buff shoved the knife in his back pocket.

Two hours later, Clay Hodges and Buff Lamb had their confessions. The former convicts had met Edith Mae (Tillie) Spoon, thirty-nine, in a bar in Klamath Falls, Oregon. After a few hours of heavy drinking, the trio took a road trip. Thirty minutes later, the married woman fell asleep, so the two kept driving.

For the next few days, the three partied and drank heavily while they made their way southeast across the United States. In Missouri, the two ex-cons stated they had tried to wake the woman and couldn't, so they pulled the car over. Only then did they discover Edith was dead!

Being former convicts, the men panicked. They straightened the woman out in the back seat and placed a blanket over her, hoping it looked like she was sleeping. They spent the next 16 hours looking for a place to dump her body.

When they came to Ozark and found the open drainage ditch next to the exchange, they intended to bury her, but they hadn't counted on Marshal Lamb thwarting their plans.

"Do you believe them, Teebob?"

"I dunno Guff, but we'll know what she died of after John (Dean) Harris' autopsy!"

Four days later, on a Friday morning, the coroner came back with a finding. Edith Mae Spoon had died of alcohol consumption and quinine poisoning. She had overdosed on alcohol. [24]Aaron Dean and James Meek had told the truth.

They set the two men free and the woman's husband, Glen Spoon, from Oregon, claimed her body. In her hometown of Klamath Falls, the paper reported that Edith had died of a heart attack while in a moving vehicle. She was "allegedly on her way to visit relatives out east." But that is not the way it happened.

Ozark, Missouri, was not the sleepy little village that many people believed it to be.

A month later, down at Linden, 13 miles from Ozark, the county learned [25]Homer A. Hatten, committed suicide. Hatten had written western novels read by fans across the country.

The next day back in Ozark, roosters crowed, dogs barked, and the morning's wash hung on clotheslines across backyards. Life never took a day off in Christian County, and neither did crime.

Sheriff Hodges arrested 65-year-old George Harp in January for selling moonshine (homemade whiskey). Harp had to post a $1,500 bond to get out of jail. Clay was not a drinking man, but occasionally, Buff slipped down to Chadwick to share a drink of homemade brew. For sore throats and such.

October 1955, Christian County lost another long-time icon. Former sheriff Elijah "Lige" Reed passed away. Lige had been the sheriff when Buff first came to Ozark in 1945.

Lige had worked for sheriff Newt Mapes in the early 1930s.

---

[24] Aaron V. Dean died five years later in the state of Kansas. He was 47.
[25] Hatten over-dosed on sleeping pills.

During those years, he had become involved in a manhunt and shooting.

Former sheriff Lige Reed died at age 70. Buff and Clay attended his funeral. Buff and Lige were both from Kentucky.

On a wintry day in November 1955, a local hell-raiser stirred things up in Christian County. Fresh out of the military, he was a Kansas tornado blowing toward Clay Hodges and Marshal Buff Lamb.

Reggie Lee Loomis, a 21-year-old Chadwick native, got drunk and crashed his car into a ditch. No big deal, but it didn't end there. With a dented fender dragging the ground, and the hood of his car still up, the Chadwick bad boy drove into Sparta.

No one could believe what they were seeing. It looked like the car had taken a wrong turn off a demolition derby track.

Once in Sparta, the ex-soldier swerved and drove his jalopy into a tree, disabling it. That should have been the end, but good old Reggie was just getting started!

His body still fueled by alcohol, Reggie grabbed a bottle of wine from the front seat, and out of the car, he went. Outside his car, Reggie stumbled over to another car that sat in front of the drugstore.

With [26]Mrs. Donald Foley sitting in the passenger's seat. Loomis broke the window and attempted to grab Mrs. Foley. Fearing for her life, Mrs. Foley broke free and ran into the drugstore and called Sheriff Hodges.

"Son of a bit...!" yelled Loomis as he drunkenly attempted to steal another car but failed. Several business owners stepped out of their stores. The dark-headed man stumbled around in the street, but no one offered to stop him.

Loomis spotted a truck in front of the MFA store and swung himself over to it. He got in it and drove west out of town. [27]Lenvil Gideon, a friend of Loomis, drove after his friend to stop him.

By the time Sheriff Hodges and Deputy Ben Hart arrived in Sparta, Loomis had managed to get himself out of town. Moments later, Sheriff Hodges received a message. There was a robbery

---

[26] Mrs. Donald Foley (Barbara) was the wife of Baptist Pastor Donald G. Foley of Sparta.
[27] Lenvil passed away on December 16, 1999. He had worked as a drywall installer.

suspect at Francis Henry's Tavern in Highlandville. The sheriff and Ben Hart rushed to Highlandville, where they arrested [28]Cecil Gold.

"Guff 101? Can you meet me at Henry's Tavern in Highlandville?"

"Yes sir, Sheriff".

Buff Lamb met Clay in Highlandville and drove the sheriff back to Sparta. They heard Loomis wrecked the pickup and that Gideon took him back to Sparta.

When drugstore owner [29]Wade Layton caught sight of Loomis, he leveled a shotgun at Loomis and fired. Breaking into cars and terrorizing women in town meant one thing; Loomis had to be put down like a rabid dog!

Luckily for Loomis, someone deflected the shotgun, and Layton's shot went high. Otherwise, Loomis would have been dead in the street and Mr. Layton may have gone to jail. A few minutes later Clay and Buff arrived.

"*Get in the car boy!*" ordered Marshal Lamb. "You make one move and I'll bring you back here and let Mr. Layton fill you full of holes! You're going to jail and you're going to pay for all the damage you caused here. *You hear me boy?*"

"Yes sir, deputy dawg!" By now, young Reggie Loomis was sobering up, but his attitude was surly.

"Watch your mouth, boy, or I will put the heel of my boot right through your chest!" After that, Loomis kept his mouth shut.

The wanna-be-criminal from Chadwick had finally met up with the Lion of the Ozarks. But his trouble-making days were far from over. When Loomis drank, he was crazier than a run over dog. He was his own worst enemy. The next few years would prove to everyone how crazy Loomis could get. This would be one of many rides in a patrol car for Reggie Loomis.

---

[28] Cecil would have more run-ins with the law. Mostly for driving while intoxicated and reckless driving. Cecil passed away with another man while sitting in a car that had become mired in the mud. With the exhaust clogged with mud, the two died of asphyxiation. He was only 47 years old.

[29] Wade had been in poor health the past few years. In 1969, Mr. Layton shot and killed himself. His wife was in the other room ironing at the time and believed he died because of his constant poor health.

Old Sparta Drugstore

CHAPTER FIVE

MURDERED FOR NO REASON

Cecil Brayfield Jr. was a 25-year-old dishwasher at the K & K Sandwich Shop in Springfield, Missouri. He was the father of five children and husband to Betty. In 1956, Brayfield finished a two-year bid at the Missouri State Penitentiary. The charge was stealing an expensive camera. As an ex-convict, Brayfield found it hard to find employment.

On a Monday afternoon in March 1956, Brayfield awakened from a night's slumber. He was tired of watching his family starve because of the mistakes he had made. He wanted money, and he wanted it quick.

Springfield authorities were familiar with Brayfield, so he drove to Ozark. Leaving his apartment, Brayfield grabbed his .32 caliber pistol. He opened the cylinder to check for bullets and snapped it shut.

Coy Tim Stumpff's parents ran an ice cream and tourist court in Ozark. Eighteen-year-old Coy Tim got a job working at Neil William's Service Station. It was a tiny shop with a gravel parking lot and four gas pumps.

After driving into Ozark, witnesses saw Brayfield's 1951 green Ford, 4-door sedan, pull into the gas station. Brayfield walked inside, and Coy Tim followed him.

A few minutes later, the wife of the owner of the station stopped in and saw Brayfield talking to Coy Tim. As did James Richardson from Sparta, five minutes later.

After everyone left, Brayfield reached in his pants pocket for the .32 caliber pistol. He pointed it at the young attendant. The youth noticed that Brayfield had tattoos on the backs of his hands. "Open that cash register and give me what's inside!"

"Mister, we don't have much money."

Coy Tim opened the register. The recent High School graduate turned toward Brayfield with his hands in the air. That's when the ex-convict pulled the trigger and slammed two bullets in his chest. One right after the other. Coy Tim fell to the floor, dying, his heart pumping blood onto the floor. It was a cold-blooded, merciless murder of a young boy. Brayfield had killed without provocation or forethought.

Undeterred by the child he had just murdered, Brayfield reached over the counter. He grabbed $11 and fled in his car back toward Springfield. He was safe, the devil himself couldn't catch him now. Young Coy Tim was dead. Murdered at the hands of a no-good, rotten-ass stain of a human being.

Brayfield's first thought was to get rid of the pistol, so he tossed it out his window. No one would find it along the road. When he got home, he failed to tell Betty what he had done. It was no big deal. They needed money, so he picked up a few bucks. Besides, she might squeal to the cops on him.

Meanwhile, back in Ozark, they found Coy Tim's body and took it to an Ozark Hospital. How would Sheriff Hodges find the strength to tell his parents that Coy Tim was dead?

Brayfield might have gotten away with the murder if not for Clay Hodges' fast detective work. The sheriff found an eyewitness who had seen Brayfield's car in town that day. With [30]Brayfield's confession, the father of five received a life sentence in prison. The entire town mourned the loss of the 18-year-old youth. How could someone be so evil as to kill a child?

Buff had stopped at the gas station and met Coy Tim. He liked

---

[30] Brayfield's wife Betty Pearl divorced him three years later. Brayfield did not serve life in prison for the murder of Coy Tim Brayfield. They later released him, and he remarried and became a school janitor. Coy Tim's twin brother would later become a reserve deputy for Buff.

the kid and would never forget his death. Christian County was not a sleepy little burg, like some people thought. There were hungry wolves out there, seeking prey, and it was Buff's job to keep them away from Ozark.

SPEAKING OF WOLVES...

The year 1957 saw severe drought conditions in Christian County. As ponds, streams, and rivers dried up, wildlife came out of the hills and caves to search for food and water in town.

Four wolves had been spotted and trapped close to the city. Citizens worried that if the wolves came into town, they might attack a child or an old person.

While on patrol at night, Buff hoped to spot and kill one. Instead, he found two "coyotes" at Francis Henry's Café. February 20th, 1957:

"There's been a shooting at Francis Henry's place in Highlandville, Buff!"

Thanks, dispatch. At the cafe?

"Yes sir, a woman (Francis Henry's wife) called and stated someone had been shot."

"En route!"

Francis Henry, the owner, rushed out into the parking lot to meet the marshal. Buff had spoken to Frances when he arrested Cecil Gold six months earlier.

"I did it Buff, I did it! I killed him!"

"Let's go inside and have a look, Francis." The two entered the restaurant. A few minutes later, Marshal Lamb heard Sheriff Hodges' patrol car sliding to a halt in the gravel driveway.

"What's going on, Guff?"

"Francis here says he killed [31]Cotton Hedgpeth. Says he shot him in the chest with a shotgun! The body's over there; he's been shot at close range."

"Secure the shotgun in your trunk and put Francis in the patrol car. I'll interview the witnesses and find out what happened here!"

Thirty minutes earlier, Cotton Hedgpeth, Oren Ball, and Charles

---

[31] His proper name was Ward "Cotton" Hedgpeth.

Blevins had come into the café. Cotton demanded a drink. Francis's wife, Florence, explained to Cotton that they did not sell alcohol anymore, but Cotton was not listening.

"Dammit, I've gotten a drink here before and I want one now!"

Francis retrieved a shotgun from behind the counter and told Florence to get in the back.

"Get him out of here, Blevins!" stated Francis.

"Screw you Francis! I ain't going nowhere!"

"By Gawd you will or I'll...I'm too old to fight you, but I…"

Oren Ball ran over to Hedgpeth and the two wrestled with the shotgun.

"He ain't going to shoot nobody!" yelled Cotton.

"Boom!" The gun went off, blasting Hedgpeth in the left chest, knocking him five feet backward. Hedgpeth fell to the ground. He was dead when his head hit the floor. Smoke wafted from the shotgun barrels as Francis lowered the weapon to his side. You could have heard a pin drop after that.

"You killed him, Francis! You shot and killed my friend! He was just fooling around! He's dead!" exclaimed Blevins.

During the trial, Buff testified he had heard Francis say he meant to kill Cotton. But, after deliberating one hour and fifteen minutes, the jury found Henry not guilty of the shooting. The jury had concluded that Cotton's death was an accident.

Ward Cotton Hedgpeth had an arrest record in Christian and Greene County. The arrests involved Cotton drinking and causing a fight. A few people, like Buff, thought Frances intentionally killed Cotton. But a jury saw it otherwise, and they let Francis go.

After the shooting and trial, Marshal Lamb's name appeared in the local newspaper, and he grew an inch taller in everyone's eyes. Buff lamb was doing his best to hold back the wolves in the night, and it wasn't going unnoticed.

HELL BOUND...

Nine months later, troublemaker Reggie Lee Loomis was back to raising hell. Still on parole for the trouble he'd caused in Sparta, this time he raised the stakes. Loomis sat in the Christian County jail accused of kidnapping and rape.

Mrs. Fern McFadden was home alone in Sparta when Loomis walked into her house with a gun. Luckily, her children were in school and her husband was working at their Gas Station. Otherwise, Loomis may have hurt one of them.

Reggie Lee Loomis forced Mrs. McFadden into his car, stating that if she didn't go, he'd blow her brains out. He bound her hands with a belt and drove to a secluded area in the Mark Twain Forest, where he sexually assaulted her.

Several hours later, Fern's children came home from school. The house looked like someone had been fighting in it. By then, Loomis had already raped their mother before dumping her off at a grocery store in Chadwick. [32]Mrs. McFadden called the sheriff's office and was taken to a hospital.

The next day, with a description of Loomis, Sheriff Hodges received information that a man was trying to coax a Sparta schoolgirl into his car. The man told the child that her mother was sick and needed her. The man matched Loomis' description.

Deputy Thompson spotted Loomis, and after a high-speed chase, stopped his car. A .32 pistol sat in the seat next to him. A belt was later found under his seat. After taking a long drink of whiskey, and making a couple of wisecracks, Loomis was taken to the Christian County Jail.

Loomis claimed he had been drinking and didn't remember the kidnapping and rape. The jury found him guilty on both accounts and sentenced him to 17 years in prison. If Buff had been the Judge, Loomis would have had his ass beaten for the rest of his life.

*

January 1958, three children were bitten by a rabid dog, causing the town to panic. But it was Marshal Lamb who found and destroyed the dangerous menace. Buff was a hunter, having

---

[32] Fern's husband passed away 11 years later in 1968. Fern lived to the age of 89.

traveled to Canada to kill a moose. Finding a mangy, vicious dog in Ozark was easy.

Buff was a popular man in Ozark and Christian County. People liked him and admired his work as the city marshal. He was among the elite, to be invited to a bridal shower at the home of [33]John L. Pile.

Buff stood out like a black bear in a flock of white sheep at the party, but no one cared. Friends accepted him for the tough, City Marshal he had become.

Buff loved his job and Christian County. He genuinely did. His counterparts tried to paint him as a brutal enforcer, but in fact, he was an aggressive young man who took his job of protecting Ozark seriously. He loved the people of Ozark, and he loved the area. He had finally found a home. He called Ozark "his county", and vowed he'd never leave it.

As for his marriage, it suffered. At the age of 17, Knial Iorg would ride with Buff in his 1958 black Chevy patrol car. Knial's biggest thrill came when Buff told Knial to drop him off at a girl's house. Keep in mind, Buff was married at the time.

"But what if something happens, Marshal? What if they call you on the radio?"

"They won't, but if they do, just come and get me. Just drive around, everyone will think you're me".

To be seventeen and drive the Marshal's car around town? By yourself? It didn't get any better than that. At least it didn't for young [34]Knial Iorg. He'd never forget those summer nights when he was the Ozark teenage lawman.

Between hob-knobbing with the rich and influential, and chasing women, Buff found time to go fishing and hunting. He even killed a bear. His fishing partners were Missouri Trooper Joe Duncan and Mark Green.

The hunting trips ended for a while when a deadly [35]spider bite sent Buff to the hospital. Like everything else, Buff recovered and was back to earning $275 a month as City Marshal.

---

[33] John L Pile was an Ozark Publisher and the President of the Chamber of Commerce. A very important man in Ozark.

[34] Knial later became active in his community and a fireman in Springfield, Missouri

[35] Most likely a Brown Recluse Spider.

In October of '58, 23-year-old Billy Lee William stole a car from Sparta. Within two hours, Buff and Clay Hodges had him in jail. Sheriff Hodges and Buff made an excellent team. Clay was the brain and Buff was the muscle.

Service Station where Coy Tim was murdered.
Springfield News-leader News

CHAPTER SIX

SPEEDING DAYS ARE OVER

January 5, 1959, [36]Winford Esty Ellis drove into Ozark with his friend Carl Edwin Robison. It was a Monday night, and the two young men were up to no good. Cruising around town, Buff spotted the two running from a parked car. They were near the Midwest Auto Parts Store.

The pair saw Buff eyeing them, so they separated and made a run for it. They were near the Ozark Rexall Store when the marshal swooped in and stopped them. The big fellow was carrying a large screwdriver.

"What are you boys doing here this time of night?"

"Nothing, deputy. We're just minding our own business." [37]Ellis was the spokesperson. Probably because he had spent the most time in jail. Buff looked in the yahoo's car and with lightning speed drew his pistol.

"Boys, you're under arrest!"

"For what, deputy?"

---

[36] In 1954, Ellis pled guilty to burglary in Cabool, Missouri. In 1956, they sentenced Ellis to 2 years at the Algoa Reformatory. They arraigned Ellis in Springfield in October 1958 for burglaries in Springfield, and Mountain Grove, Missouri. In 1969, Ellis stole a car and was facing Federal time.

[37] Ellis was free on bond from Wright County. In a Springfield holdup, they accused Ellis of tying up a night watchman. Ellis's trouble with the law went back a couple of years.

"You've got burglar tools in your car." Again, the young one, (Ellis) looked straight at the Marshal and bravely spoke.

"What if we decide to run?"

"Please do. I'll even give you a head start. I ain't shot a skunk in a long time

"Do what he says [38]Ellis, he means it.", Robison said.

Buff had the dispatcher call the sheriff and the boys were locked up in jail. The next morning, they discovered the Midwest Auto Store had been broken into. The store was a few feet away from where Buff had arrested the two. The thieves must have run when they heard Buff approaching.

Two months later, Marshal Buff Lamb made one of his biggest captures to date. His courage and prowess as a lawman could never be questioned again. The crime began in Texas in March 1959 but would end in Ozark, Missouri, a few days later.

Everett Fulce and Joseph Everett Smallwood had planned out their robbery. They knew when to hit the home of Thomas T. Neal in Irving, Texas. Neal would be gone on jury duty, and his wife would be out of town. With luck, they'd have plenty of time to ransack the rich man's home.

The burglary went off without a hitch! Both men couldn't believe how easy it was. Of course, Smallwood had been down this road before. To his credit, he had racked up five prior felonies. Smallwood was on his way to becoming a big-time crook.

From Texas, the two traveled to Tulsa, Oklahoma, and met up with a tiny young girl who gave her age as twenty-nine. She was, in reality, only seventeen. In Tulsa, they made their biggest score. They got away with guns, pistols, furs, alcohol, and jewelry. The car was a department store on wheels. Heading north, the trio stole another sedan and crossed into Arkansas.

Two hours later they were in southern Missouri. "Here, I want you guys to have a pistol. If the cops stop us, we ain't going to jail. If I go back again, they'll probably give me life. I'd rather die in a hail of bullets first! Ain't no cop going to take me alive!"

"But I ain't never killed nobody, Joe."

"Maybe you won't have to, Everett, but hold on to the gun anyway.

---

[38] Winford Esty Ellis died at 52 in 1989.

"Damn, Everett, we're just like the Bonnie and Clyde gang! Hey, pass me one of those cigarettes!"

It was evening and the sun had set when the sedan rolled into Ozark, unaware they had just crossed into Lamb country. The most protected county in the state. The car edged into [39]John Emmett Kerr's Drive-in.

John Kerr had graduated from Ozark High School in 1926, where he played on the school's basketball team. He was active during WWII and drove a school bus in Ozark.

After watching the trio get in and out of their car, John became suspicious and called Marshal Lamb. The marshal hastily responded to the Drive-in. He hadn't [40]shaved for several days and was sporting a rough mustache and beard in preparation of Christian County's bi-centennial celebration.

"What were they doing that got your attention, John?"

"They parked over there, (pointing to the edge of the field) and kept fiddling with their car. Something was strange about those three Buff. They aren't kids."

"Did you get a description of the car?"

"Yes, it was a 1951, four-door Buick with whitewall tires."

Buff had what he needed. He radioed the dispatcher and stated he was heading south of town, and to call the Sheriff.

Buff stopped the sedan near the Dairy Queen operated by the Stumpff family. The same Stumpff family whose son had been murdered at a service station. Buff was standing behind the Buick when Sheriff Hodges arrived.

"What do you have, Guff?"

"These folks were acting suspiciously at the Drive-in. Something is not right about these people, Teebob. Look how loaded down their car and trunk is."

"Let's pull them out of the car!"

"Folks, get out of the car with your hands up!" shouted the Marshal.

The trio didn't move. It was now or never. They could shoot it out with lawmen and make a run for it, or they could give up.

---

[39] John Emmett Kerr was born in 1907 and passed away in 2004 at 96.

[40] March 8, 1959, marked a 100-year mark for Christian County. The men in town grew beards to celebrate the 3-day event. Buff was chairman of the publicity committee.

Smallwood whispered to Everett. "I ain't going back to prison. You still packin'?"

"Yes, but. . .."

The young girl spoke up. "We're getting out Sheriff!"

Their crime spree was over. Running from the law was no longer an option. They were caught. As [41]Smallwood stepped out of the car, Buff noticed he had a pistol in his waistband.

"They're armed Teebob!" Sheriff Hodges unsnapped and withdrew his pistol from its' holster. "Get their weapons, Guff!" All three were armed.

Inside the vehicle were guns, cameras, radios, television sets, jewelry, and liquor. It was the largest stolen cache either lawman had ever seen. Definitely the biggest one in Christian County.

In the Sheriff's office, Buff and Clay discovered the three had robbed E. A. Smith, an oilman in Tulsa, Oklahoma. The thieves had stolen an estimated $15,000 worth of goods. They told the lawmen that they were on their way to West Plains, Missouri.

The huge bust made headlines, making Marshal Lamb the talk of Christian County and Southwest Missouri. After all, it was Buff who answered the call and stopped the armed bandits. Both lawmen were lucky they didn't have to shoot it out with the trio. By a stroke of courageous law enforcement and luck, Buff grew another six inches in everyone's eyes.

For the next few months, no matter where he went, Marshal Lamb was treated like a celebrity. Folks had read about the car stop and were proud of their town Marshal. However; the adulations did not stop there. Buff was about to grow even taller. Springfield, the third-largest city in the state, was about to make Buff Lamb a household name.

William Howard Arwood was big for his age. At twenty-two years old, he was almost 300 pounds and 6'5 inches tall. For the past few years, Arwood had stayed in trouble with the Springfield police department. He had charges of resisting arrest, refusing to leave a nightclub and a disturbance at a Hi-Boy restaurant.

The big boy liked to drive fast, drunk, and reckless. From 1957 to 1959 he had a copious number of tickets and arrests. He had no

---

[41] Smallwood received a total sentence of 15 years. Fulce received 13. The girl was turned over to the juvenile authorities.

respect for the law and lived by his own rules. He looked down on cops as inbreds who'd never be as tough or smart as he was. But he was misguided. He had not yet met the right cop.

With a souped-up car and no respect for the law, Arwood had been running amok all year long in his 1955 sedan. On November 24th, 1959, Arwood picked up two friends in Springfield and went cruising through the town.

When Arwood drove past Springfield Police Officer Hank Crutchfield at a high rate of speed, the officer gave chase. Like he did many times before, Arwood stepped on the gas, reaching speeds of 120 miles per hour.

At those speeds, with three boys in the hotrod, Arwood would eventually crash. Crutchfield backed off the chase. Besides, he knew where the car was going. It was traveling toward Ozark.

A few minutes later, Marshal Lamb received a dispatch that Arwood was flying his way at a high rate of speed. Four minutes later, Arwood crossed the Greene\Christian County line. Now he was in Marshal Lamb's territory, and that was not a good place to be—if you were running from the law.

The City Marshal had been listening to the chase on his radio and was waiting for the speedster. He'd stop Arwood by any means necessary. The same rules in Greene County didn't apply to the rules in Christian County. They handled things differently in Ozark. Well, at least Buff Lamb did.

Stepping out onto the highway with a shotgun, Buff leveled it at his shoulder. The hotrod quickly slammed on the brakes and came to a screeching halt. "Get out of the car!" bellowed the Paul Bunyan-looking Marshal. Arwood sat there a moment, wondering if the man was going to shoot him. At this range, the shotgun blast would shatter the windshield and possibly kill one or two of them. The marshal sounded serious. His two friends were begging him to get out, but Arwood didn't want to.

"He won't shoot us! He can't. He's a cop."

"I've heard things about this guy, Bill. They say he ain't right in the head! Someone said he killed a guy down in Texas. Let's get out. *Please*!"

"I'm getting out, don't shoot! Don't shoot!" said Arwood. Maybe his friend was right.

Buff put his shotgun in his left hand. He walked up to the young man and snatched Arwood by the collar with his [42]plate-sized right hand. "Your running days are over boy, now get in that patrol car!"

According to public records, [43]Arwood was fined $350. The following year, in 1960, Arwood was in a dance club in Springfield when he was hit on the head with a beer bottle. Arwood had refused to stop dancing with another man's wife.

Arwood wasn't the only man with a lead foot. Another fellow learned crossing into Christian County at a high rate of speed was a bad idea. High School Senior, Knial Iorg, was riding with Buff the night another man thought he could fly past the law.

"We were backed in at the Texaco Station when Buff received a dispatch. They said a man from Illinois was headed our way at a high rate of speed. Buff eased out of the station and drove onto the highway. Buff grabbed a shotgun, and we both got out. Buff stood out on the highway. I backed up, not knowing what to expect."

"A few minutes later we saw headlights, and the man saw Buff in the middle of the road with the shotgun. By now, I was far away from Buff. I didn't know what was going to happen! The man hit his brakes, and the car came to a squalling stop a few feet in front of Buff. I did not know if Buff was brave or stupid. He could have been killed! Well, Buff jerked that man out of the car and worked him over pretty good. Afterward, he took him to jail."

Most of the citizens already knew it, but for those who didn't, the word spread. If you were up to mischief; go somewhere else, but not in Christian County. Buff was a big man with a big reputation in southwest Missouri.

---

[42] Stan Shelton remembered that Buff's hands were so big that he would have to bait his hook because Buff kept smashing the minnows.

[43] Arwood passed away at 81 in Springfield, Missouri.

CHAPTER SEVEN

RUN FOR SHERIFF

The Army dishonorably discharged Raymond Louis Smith in the state of Illinois. The charges against him are unclear. What we do know is, the twenty-two-year-old hitchhiked to Michigan, then south to Springfield, Missouri. Smith tried to find work, but had no luck. So, he robbed a store, but he did it using skills they had taught him in the Army. He scouted his target before attacking.

Smith went to a grocery store in Springfield, every day for three days. He entered the store and bought a 10-cent soda and spent the next few hours watching the cashier. To make his plan work, he needed to catch the cashier alone in the store. He succeeded on the third day.

Smith grabbed the cashier by her wrist and told her, "This is a hold-up!" The ex-soldier left with $60.00 to $100.00 cash. Smith headed for the railroad tracks, ditched his light-colored shirt, then went east to Highway 65. From Springfield, Smith hitchhiked and was picked up by a carload of boys headed to Ozark early the next morning.

Buff looked down at his watch. It was 2:15 am when he stopped the Studebaker. Why would nine kids pack themselves in a car like sardines this early in the morning? They could only be up to no good. Thirty minutes earlier, he'd received a dispatch. Some boys had robbed the Salzman Market in Springfield on St. Louis Street.

Buff got all the boys out of the car. It looked like a college frat house alongside the road. Two of the boys matched the robbers description and could not verify their whereabouts. Those two, he took to jail.

In the courthouse, Buff discovered Smith still had thirty-dollars stuffed into the toe of one shoe. After some pressure from the big marshal, Smith relented and confessed to the robbery.

Smith received the maximum. A year in jail for stealing. On December 12, 1960, Smith attempted an escape in Springfield but was captured. Raymond Louis Smith was later granted a parole in March 1961.

By the time of this arrest, Buff had made more and bigger arrests than any other City Marshal before him. Next to Sheriff Hodges, Buff was the biggest lawman in the county. His name was spreading into Greene, Taney, Douglas, Webster, and Stone counties, just in time for the 1960 Christian County Sheriff's race.

"Buff, I'm not running for sheriff this time, and I want you to take my place in the Sheriff's office."

"But what about Rex Thompson? He's your deputy, and he says he's going to run."

"Rex is good, but I've known you a lot longer. This county needs a man who won't back down from trouble. Besides, Rex is running as a Democrat. This county is Republican!"

Buff paused and then quietly spoke. "You know I want to be Sheriff, Teebob."

"I can help you get elected. The biggest problem I see is Jack Monger. You know Jack's father Joe was the sheriff right before me."

"Is he running?"

"I was at the Barber Shop, and they said he was."

Jack Anderson Monger served as a Marine in the Philippines from 1944 to 1946. When he came back, he operated an insurance business in Ozark. He played golf and was the local chairman of the Red Cross.

Jack was affable and liked by everyone. A man you wanted as your neighbor or deacon at your church. He was a man you could trust, and was well known throughout the County. He had the Monger's name which would come in very handy during an election.

Experience would go to Buff, but the ability to make people feel at ease would go to Jack Monger.

Four months later, Captain Frank Lovell joined the race. Lovell had served in the Korean War. He received the following Medals: The Combat Service Medal, Bronze Star, Combat Infantry Medal, and a Good Conduct Medal. After the war, he became an auctioneer, pastor, and 10-month deputy of Clay Hodges.

Buff had never spent a day in the military. His brother Carter had, but not Buff. Conceivably because of all the injuries he sustained as a Daredevil.

Back on the home front, Buff was facing domestic problems. His constant womanizing had caused Ruby Jo to leave him and move to [44]Republic, Missouri. Buff could not leave the women alone.

He was also scaring his ex-wife, Mary Lee, and two children. Buff would park his car and watch his children play in the yard. Worried that Buff may try to kidnap them, Mary Lee would take the children inside and hide them. Her opinion of Buff was less than worthy of a man running for Sheriff or any office.

With a cloud of physical abuse and infidelity hanging over his head, Buff's divorce to Ruby Jo was imminent. Buff had no problems getting a woman, but like grasping water, they seemed impossible to hold onto.

The marriage separation came as a crippling blow to Buff's political aspirations. People in a small-town talk, and Buff's personal life was on the street like Wednesday's wash.

"How many times has the Marshal been married, Norma?"

"I heard six!"

"Oh no, Blanche! It's five! Isn't that what you heard Wilma?"

"I heard he married Mary Lee twice and still sees her on the side!"

"Goodness gracious! What is wrong with that man? And the gall of him wanting to be our sheriff!"

"Abner Dooley said Barney Wilson caught him out with his

---

[44] Ruby Jo moved to Republic and opened a restaurant. She called it "Jo's Place".

wife and the two shot it out! And later that night, the two went drinking at the Bucket of Blood!"

The malicious talk came at an inopportune time. Buff had not been in a shootout, but he had been [45]married 4 times. Buff hoped these back-fence conversations would not turn the election against him. But they did.

August 1960, insurance man, and all-around nice guy, Jack Monger, won the position of Sheriff. He beat Buff by 741 votes. The county had spoken. Charismatic and engaging, Jack Monger was the Christian County Sheriff.

"Sorry you lost the election, [46]Buff. I was sure they'd pick you!" said Missouri State Trooper Jerry Hart. "I've known you and Clay for a long time. Sorry to hear you lost."

"That's okay, Jerry. The worst part is, Ruby Jo and I are getting divorced. When it rains, it pours!"

"What happened?"

"She said she lost interest in the marriage and didn't care about me anymore! She moved out, and I let her go."

Three days later, December 11th, 1960, Buff and Ruby Jo [47]divorced. Buff paid Ruby Jo $300 for the equity in their home, and in return, Ruby Jo signed over a quick claim deed to their property.

Four months after his divorce, Buff attended a ceremony with city leaders. In attendance was newly elected Mayor, Donald Chaffin, Sheriff Monger, and Buff... with his fifth wife, Louella Gardner. The two had married earlier that day, and the proud husband introduced her to all his friends.

"Buff changes wives more than I change my underwear!" Exclaimed Ernie Turlet.

Jack Monger turned out to be a good Sheriff. Monger preferred people's respect by showing kindness and honesty. Law enforcement didn't always come at the end of a nightstick or the

---

[45] If you count Mary Lee, who he married twice.
[46] Buff came in 3rd behind Captain F. Lovell.
[47] The marriage to Ruby Jo lasted less than 8 Years.

butt end of a pistol. Monger wanted people to honor the law, not fear it.

MONGER GRABS HEADLINES WHILE SHERIFF

"Girl Turns Herself into Human Torch"

After an argument with her sister, 17-year-old Linda Moore of Ozark went outside and poured gasoline all over her body and lit a match. Linda's screams brought the young girl's mother and three sisters into the yard to see what the matter was. Marion Moore, Linda's mother, ripped off Linda's flaming clothes, but not before the fire burned 85 percent of Linda's body.

"Missourian Sets Up Elaborate Method to Take His Own Life"

Suicidal Adron Clarence Gideon climbed down into a cave and rigged a shotgun to blast himself into eternity by tossing a rock tied to the gun's trigger. However, before he tossed the rock, he swallowed a half bottle of sleeping pills. The pills killed the former janitor before he could toss the rock. Learning of Gideon's whereabouts, it was Sheriff Monger who climbed down into the cave and discovered the body.

March 1961 Sheriff Monger and Buff Lamb arrested the infamous [48]"Buttermilk Johnson". I could write a book about the notorious Buttermilk. Everyone in Ozark knew him.

Buff would get another run at sheriff, but before that, he would have to prove he was as tough as people said he was. Like always, Buff Lamb was up to the challenge. Buff walked the walk and he talked the talk. Buff didn't think he was tough; he knew he was!

---

[48] Wayne "Buttermilk" Johnson held the record as the most arrested person in Christian County, Missouri. A pre-sentence investigation revealed that Buttermilk had been arrested 198 times since 1939. Nothing too serious, mind you, mostly drunkenness, train jumping, vagrancy, and peace disturbance. Supposedly, he once commandeered a microphone at a rodeo and began singing to the crowd on it. Springfield once let Buttermilk go on the promise that he would not return to town and do his drinking only in Christian County!

CHAPTER EIGHT

GO BACK IN YOUR HOUSE AND HIDE

Jack Hightower lived in Kansas City, where he had a reputation as a tough guy. He could have been connected to organized crime. No one knows for sure. But before 1964, the name Buff Lamb had reached his ears.

Like a gunfighter from the old west, seeking to make a reputation for himself, Hightower drove to Ozark to challenge the town marshal. Whipping a City Marshal, who everyone regarded as the toughest man in southwest Missouri, would do a lot for his notoriety. One afternoon Hightower arrived in Ozark and knocked on Buff's door.

"Who is it, Luella?"

"Some man says he wants to talk to you, Buff." Buff walked to the door in a tee-shirt and jeans.

"What can I do for you, mister?"

"I hear you're that ass-hole marshal who has everyone in this town afraid of him!"

"Get the hell out of here. I don't have time for you!"

"I didn't think you were so tough! Go back in your house and hide behind your wife's skirts. I knew it was just tough talk!"

The man turned and walked away but heard a screen door slam and turned around. It was Buff, standing off the front porch.

"You wanna find out how tough I am? Come on, you son-of-a-bitch!" And the two men fought in Buff's front yard.

"When it was over, Jack Hightower (name withheld) had to crawl back to his car. Buff beat him so bad he could not stand up. I know it is true because I knew the man and he told me about it later," said a former lawman.

"Everything they said about Buff being tough—was true," said a [49]man who was friends with Buff and Hightower.

Buff was no fool. He knew someone had sent for the Kansas City gorilla, but who? And what was the purpose? To put him in his place? It didn't matter, they could send whoever they wanted. He'd take on anyone they sent. The ones he couldn't whip, he'd use a 2x4, a flashlight, or the butt end of a revolver. No matter what, they would not get his badge.

At the end of 1963, it was time to make another run for sheriff. However, on December 6th, the 39-year-old marshal suffered a heart attack, proving he was not superhuman after all. But it would take more than a minor heart attack to keep Buff Lamb down. Buff spent a few days in the hospital, then returned to his uniform and night patrol.

Buff announced his candidacy for sheriff on January 30th of 1964. Running against him was Billy Joe Sisco. Sisco had more law enforcement experience than Buff, making him more qualified for the job.

For instance, Sisco was a former War Veteran, Christian County Deputy, Springfield Police Officer, Greene County Deputy, and Rockaway Beach Police Officer. Buff had been a Bull Rider, Daredevil, and City Marshal.

Sisco believed he had an excellent chance of winning. His only obstacles were Sheriff Jack Monger and Marshal Buff Lamb. Buff walked tall and had proven he was a tough lawman. People respected Buff. And no one could question how tough he was. If you were facing a fight, you wanted Buff Lamb on your side.

Sisco's motto was "Building Boys Is Better Than Mending Men". On his election poster, he stated that he had been married only "one time". His running mate Buff had wed five times.

Both men attended pancake breakfasts, and chili suppers. They

---

[49] This man was a former law enforcement officer with Buff.

spoke at women's meetings and knocked on doors. Additionally, Buff worked the streets of Ozark and answered county calls for help. Sisco had the experience, but Buff had popularity and a renowned reputation.

On a Tuesday night in March, about 9 pm, marshal was making his rounds when he received a dispatch. Two men had stolen a car in Springfield from the Calvary Temple Church on West Grand Street. They described the car as a 1953 Chevrolet.

Driving past a service station, Buff saw a car matching the stolen car's description, and it contained two men answering the thieves' descriptions.

Eyeing the Marshal, the two men jumped in their car and slowly drove down a dead-end road. They stopped in front of the Ozark Cemetery and turned out their lights. But it was too late, the Marshal was on their trail.

Buff eased his car down the road and stopped. "Get out of the car, boys, and show me some identification". Sure enough, he had nabbed the car thieves.

Buff's arrest made it into the Christian County Republican Newspaper for all to see. Perfect timing with an election just around the corner. As for the two car thieves, one of them, Cecil Wayne Roberts, received a year in the Greene County Jail. Roberts escaped the next month from a road gang. In fact, Roberts would escape from custody several times in the future.

August 4, 1964, Buff won the Republican Sheriff Primary. He beat out Jack Monger, and Billy Joe Sisco. He beat Billy, by 528 votes. Sisco was not happy. He quickly filed to run as an independent candidate.

Unfortunately, [50]Mary Lee Hursh, Buff's third wife, filed for back child support for $3,950. The filing came in October 1964, giving Buff the appearance of a dead-beat dad. And to be honest, he was. Child support was something Mary Lee provided for the children, not Buff.

The suit made the local newspaper, and a smile embraced Billy Sisco's face. Who would elect a sheriff that was behind on his child support? No one, that's who.

November of '64 all the votes were cast, and Christian County

---

[50] Mary Lee had married Llyod D. Hursh on February 12th, 1955.

had elected a new Sheriff. His name? Louard Elbert (Buff) Lamb. Billy Sisco was wrong. Buff had beaten [51]Sisco in the primary and then beat him again in the election. Now it was time to make Christian County a safer place to live, and Buff was eager to get started.

Marshal Lamb for Sheriff

---

[51] Billy Joe Sisco died at 69. He had retired from Zenith in Springfield as a Security Guard.

CHAPTER NINE

NEW SHERIFF IN TOWN

Besides Buff, 1964 saw several new Southwest Missouri Sheriffs elected. Former professional Baseball Catcher [52]Mickey Owen, in Greene County (Springfield). Sheriff Lyman Cardwell in Taney County (Forsyth). Lyman had been a former school bus driver and chief of police for two years. Both men were first-term Sheriffs and would play an integral part in Buff's life.

Also elected was [53]Buford Hayes Pusser in Tennessee. For the rest of his life, Buff would be compared to the hard-nosed sheriff who cleaned up McNairy County, Tennessee.

The first order of business? Sheriff Lamb swore in three new deputies. Former mentor Clay Hodges would be responsible for office duties and Bailiff. [54]James (J. B.) Casey of Chadwick, and [55]William (Bill) Lawrence of Clever, patrolmen. Casey would be Buff's Chief Deputy.

Next, Buff created "Squad 15". This group of reserve deputies

---

[52] Sheriff Owens also served in the Navy during WWII.

[53] During his lifetime, Buford became a legend in McNairy County. Much like Buff in Christian County, Missouri.

[54] J. B. moved to Ozark from Arkansas in December 1964.

[55] Bill Lawrence was a big man and a good deputy.

would be used in times of emergencies. Men like Everett Ball, Gale Clinton, Kenny Young, and Bill McKnabb. These men could be trusted and called upon to have his back.

After squad 15, Buff had [56]Mike Crain fashion some pine billyclubs to hand out to his men.

"After breaking a few clubs (from offenders resisting arrest) Crain re-made the [57]sticks, a former deputy said. This time they were made out of oak.

When Sheriff Buff Lamb pinned on his badge, he became the most powerful man in Christian County. More powerful than the Mayor, Judge, City Council, and Prosecutors.

As County Sheriff, citizens provisioned Buff with the authority to dispense justice. According to "his" interpretation of the law. When, and if, he saw fit.

"Buff was the best guy I ever worked for," said [58]Chief Deputy J.B. Casey. "He looked out for us and gave us a day off if we needed it. If you broke the law and did what he told you to do, there wouldn't be a problem. But if you didn't, Buff could get rough. I remember this one time a Highway Patrolman caught a man and needed him locked up in Buff's jail;"

"You're Buff Lamb, aren't you?" exclaimed the arrested man.

"Yes, I am."

"I think I'll just whip you!"

"You don't want to do that, sit back down." The man sat down momentarily but bounced back up quickly.

"Nope, I think I'll just whip you instead."

"That wouldn't be wise. Sit down and shut up." The man sat down, but a few seconds later got back to his feet again.

"I think I'm gonna whip you! — Bam!"

"Buff hit the man and knocked him flat on his back. The loudmouth was out cold! Buff grabbed him by his heels and dragged him to a jail cell. When Buff told you to do something, *you did it!*"

---

[56] Mike Crain and his brother owned Native Wood Products in Ozark. Mike lived to be 82 years old.

[57] Former Deputy Dale Reynolds showed me (this writer) a "head-knocker" Buff had given him made from a hedge apple tree.

[58] I interviewed James Casey on January 8th, 2017. He is a smart and kind man. James retired from the Post Office after a total of 34 years.

Buff had not been in office a full month when Deputy Bill Lawrence called him late one night.

"101 I think you'd better get down here!"

"What do you have Bill?"

"A burned-up car." "Anyone in it?"

"Nope, but I believe the car is stolen."

"101 in route!"

The 1963 Chevrolet was stolen. Taken from Thompsons Car Lot in Springfield on December 13th, 1964. Stripped of all its useful parts. Afterward, they soaked the car with gasoline and set it on fire.

A few days later, Buff arrested a juvenile, who in return, surrendered the men who had torched the car. Buff paid them a visit and arrested them at gunpoint. The suspects stole cars, stripped them, and burned them to destroy any evidence.

March 1965, Buff received word that two wanted car thieves were staying at a Motel in Ozark. The trio had warrants out of St. Louis, Missouri.

"J. B. go get [59]Jack and call the Highway Patrol. I just received word that several suspicious characters are staying at the Motel on the edge of town. I believe they might be a couple of car thieves!"

Just before midnight, Buff knocked on the couple's door.

"I'm Sheriff Buff Lamb and I need you to open up! I need to talk to you!". A young man came to the door.

"What can I do for you Sheriff?"

"Is that your car over there?"

"I guess so, what business is it of yours?"

"The car's been stolen, smart mouth! You and your girlfriend are under arrest."

The two rode in Buff's patrol car to the Sheriff's office. Once there, the lawmen discovered that the trio had been stealing cars out of St. Louis. From there, they'd sell them in Springfield. Sometimes they'd get as much as $1,600 per car.

"Good work Buff," said the Highway Patrolmen. "Anytime you need us, call us!"

Buff had the respect of most lawmen in the southern part of the state.

---

[59] Jack Cornog, Ozark City Marshal.

Early in April, Buff received word that a group of kids were drinking down at Lindenlure. Buff had made a promise to voters; "he would curb underage drinking."

"J.B go pick up Russell (Heatherly). We're headed to Lindenlure. Tell him to bring his car. We may need it."

Deputy Casey did as he was told and the three caravanned over to Linden bridge. Ten youths were taken in for underage drinking. Buff was keeping his promise to the county.

In June, Buff arrested Dorothy Lloyd at the Hilltop Liquor Store for selling alcohol to a minor.

Also arrested, were two men who had kidnapped two boys, stripped them, and then locked them in the trunk of their car. The men were arrested by the Nixa Marshal and two of Buff's deputies.

Thirty-six hours later, Buff was injured in a car accident on his way to a wreck. No stranger to pain, Buff was transported in an ambulance to have a doctor look at his knee. It was swollen and he thought he might have broken something.

Buff Lamb was no ordinary man. From his jaw to his ankles, he had broken his bones. It was a miracle he could stand or walk. Too many car crashes, motorcycle jumps, fights, and angry bulls. And now he was experiencing the pains of middle age. Lucky for him, the department had gained new helpers.

"Buff loved dogs. When Greene County Sheriff Mickey Owen offered them to him... He took 'em! The bloodhound they called "Beauty" and the Shepard, they called "Domino".

"We used the dogs for tracking and finding missing persons". Said former deputy Russell Heatherly.

One former deputy recalled the time a man escaped from jail and Buff used the dogs. Beauty and Domino tracked the escapee to the Finley River. That's where they found him cold and hanging onto some branches in the water. If not for the dogs, the man might have escaped.

"The dogs could be a problem." Recalled Deputy Heatherly. "I believe it was Domino who cost the county some money. Domino was scared to death of storms. One night, Buff left him in his car during a thunderous storm. Man, that dog tore Buff's car up! He shredded those seats with his claws, trying to get out! That car was completely torn apart on the inside!"

Wilma Cantrell, sister of Jackie Cornog, the town marshal, once gave Buff a dog. "It was [60]mean, and I couldn't afford to feed it! I told Buff about it and he said he'd take it. Buff said he wanted a mean dog! I had the dog on a rope in the backyard and told Buff to be careful when he went back there to get it. I thought the dog might bite him.

Buff went back there, and I followed him. Buff looked at it, cursed it, untied the rope, and took the dog home. And you know what? Buff kept that dog until the day he (dog) died!" The dogs were on hand in July of that year in the tourist town of Rockaway Beach.

Nestled in the southern hills of Missouri, along Lake Taneycomo, sits the town of Rockaway Beach. Built as a tourist attraction in the early 1900s, to get to Rockaway, you traveled by train and then by boat.

By the early 1920s, Willard Merriam encouraged Springfieldians to visit Rockaway. Merriam stated they could drive their "machines" to the resort.

Willard Merriam sold lots on Lake Taneycomo in the town in 1923. He advertised fishing, hunting, boating, hiking, and swimming. Al Capone stayed at the resort in the 1930s.

By 1960, the resort town relied on the business of tourists and vacationers. Young men and women flooded the streets of Rockaway Beach on holidays, the same as they did in Branson, Missouri. They enjoyed the lakeshore, and could walk from tavern to tavern, arcade to arcade, and back to their hotels and cottages.

But all that changed on Independence Day, July 4th, 1965. What happened next would make headlines across the nation. And Sheriff Buff Lamb would be in the middle of it.

---

[60] Buff often used a mean German Shepard dog named Coco to break up parties along the river. Kim Owens recalled the dog belonged to Bud Holman.

Squad 15

Louella (Gardner) Lamb, Buff Lamb, Bill Lawrence and Tom Padgett

CHAPTER TEN

ROCKAWAY THE NIGHT

They started rolling into Rockaway Beach on Friday, July 2nd, 1965. They came from Missouri, Kansas, and Illinois. Hundreds of them, most between the ages of eighteen and twenty-four, and they all had one thing in common--they were there to party!

As Deputy Marshal [61]Pletcher Rogers, the only law in town made his rounds, temperatures hovered around the 80-degree mark.

Saturday, July 3rd, the town with a capacity of 5,000 had been injected with 7,000–8,000 tourists. One report had motorcycles being brought in by the truckloads.

Ray Weter and some friends had seen Pletcher in Sparta. The Rockaway Marshal warned them; "Stay out of Rockaway Beach, boys. It's a mess down there."

Rumor had it, for the past few years, a tourist could carouse and openly drink on the streets during the holidays. [62]Rowdiness was expected and overlooked by law enforcement and business owners.

---

[61] Pletcher would have a lengthy career in Law Enforcement and municipal politics. He even ran against Buff Lamb in a Sheriff's election.

[62] Reminiscent of the old cattle towns in the west. The town turned a blind eye toward minor crimes.

"Last season, Rocco ([63]Carlo Rocco Schiavone) told me that if I didn't slacken up on the young people, they might find me on one of the docks in the lake with a rock around my neck...I have been hooted and jeered," said Marshal Pletcher Rogers. Rocco owned the Gay 90s tavern, and if he wanted you dead, he had the means to make it happen.

With overcrowding came the inability to park cars. The newcomers parked on the boulevard sidewalks and wandered the streets, most of them with open beer bottles or whiskey.

On the hill above the boulevard stretched hillside cabins and motels, over half of them stacked full of cases of beer. One man brought in thirty-five cases of beer to sell to the tourists from the back seat and trunk of his car.

The town was a powder keg with drug activity, open sex, and young people looking for excitement. With only one cop on duty. All the ingredients for a pending disaster were falling into place.

Things took a turn for the worse when Marshal Rogers received word of a shooting at the drugstore. Pletcher rushed down the street to investigate.

Meanwhile, more officers arrived to help with the crowd. When Rogers returned, he spoke to Deputy Sheriff Bill Sisco. Bill told him he and Police Commissioner, [64]Bill Booth, had arrested three boys that were riding a motorcycle all at the same time. The boys were drunk and weaving through the crowd.

Around midnight, Rocco closed his club, and hundreds of imbibed partygoers spilled onto the streets. Looking for excitement and mischief, the mob shouted obscenities. They pushed, shoved, and sloshed drinks everywhere.

Word spread that the local cops had arrested three boys for no reason. Within ten minutes, over five-hundred agitators surrounded the jail. The crowd began hurling rocks, insults, firecrackers, and boards at the jail.

"*Let those boys out*! Come on pigs, let them out! Either you let them out or we'll come in and get them! *We'll tear this town apart!*"

Don Meston from St. Louis was there and saw the arrest this

---

[63] Carlos was once described as "Armenian, and very East Coast-ish".
[64] Bill Booth owned Naoti's Restaurant at Green Mountain Lodge.

way: "The police pulled these kids off a motorcycle and started to take them to jail. Everyone began throwing fireworks and bottles at the policemen. The kids were horsing around at first, but that seemed to get them started."

Like the Ozark Mountains around them, the lawmen weren't about to move. It was a classic scene from a twentieth-century western movie. Six lone lawmen holding their prisoners against an angry mob. But unlike the movies, this was real, and they outnumbered the lawmen over a thousand to one.

Meanwhile, outside the [65]jail, the crowd demanded the release of the two boys. Two minutes later, it started. Officer [66]Pletcher Rogers could hear glass breaking further down the strip. The odor of something burning filled his nostrils. Pletcher and another police officer exited the jail.

Shoving his way through the crowd, Pletcher found himself surrounded by unhinged degenerates. They had one thing in mind; hassle the cops and let them know "they" were in control of the town.

At one point, the drugged and inebriated delinquents surrounded Pletcher. He was one man against a mob. The rabble threatened to place a cinder block around his neck and drown him in the lake. Maybe it was fear, anger, or a combination of both, but Rogers stood up to the mob and pushed his way through.

By now Sheriff Lyman Cardwell of Forsyth had arrived and walked down to the jail. After seeing what had transpired over the past hour, he headed down to his patrol car. He found his car window had been busted out, and the radio's microphone was missing. Cardwell turned toward deputy Bill Sisco and told him to make a call.

"Call it in, Bill. We need help down here. These people are going to tear this town apart!"

Word went out to every Law Enforcement agency across Southwest Missouri received a dispatch requesting additional manpower in Rockaway Beach. "If help doesn't arrive soon, there won't be a Rockaway Beach!" stated the dispatcher.

---

[65] The jail was between a liquor store and a service station on Beach Boulevard.
[66] This was Pletcher's 2nd year as a law enforcement officer. Sheriff Joe Mayberry had asked Pletcher to take the job.

"Ray, get in with me! They're rioting in Rockaway Beach! We've got to get down there!" said Buff.

Ozark Chief of Police, Ray Speak, jumped into the sheriff's patrol car and the two sped off for Rockaway Beach, twenty-seven miles south of Ozark. With red lights and sirens blaring, they cut through the summer darkness, hoping to find the officers alive and unharmed, the resort town intact.

In the back seat was one of Buff's dogs. The canine whined like it knew something exciting was about to happen.

Back in Rockaway, rioters overturned a police car. The crowd, now 8,000 strong, had turned into a plague of swarming malcontents. If help didn't arrive soon, they would destroy the town and its forty businesses. As for the officers, it was doubtful they would survive.

"Pletcher Rogers is down there, isn't he, Buff?".

"Yeah. They're calling for anyone who can help." Twenty minutes later, the law dogs drove out of the hills and looked over at Rockaway.

"*Son-of-a-bitch*! Look at that crowd, Ray!"

There were cars everywhere! Bumper to bumper down the entire street. No one was moving anywhere. From their vantage point, Buff and Ray could see people stealing from cars and throwing beer bottles. A group of troublemakers had assembled on the roofs of the buildings. Anyone wearing a badge was a target.

Further down the street they could hear what sounded like [67]gunfire or fireworks in the distance.

Twenty yards away, Buff and Ray saw an overturned patrol car. The town was flooded with young bodies, all appearing to be twenty-five or younger. Signs were ripped off of poles, windows busted out. and trash all over the streets. Buff looked over at Ray. "Watch your back, Ray, this may get ugly!"

"Buff stepped out with a double-barreled shotgun in his right hand and the dog's leash in the other. He was in his element, turmoil, civil insurrection, and chaos. Buff loved this kind of crap! "If he was afraid, he didn't show it!" said Ray Speaks.

---

[67]A few people were hit with buckshot while store owners protected their property.

[68]Russell Heatherly, a Lamb deputy, arrived a few minutes after Buff. He, too, got out of a patrol car with a dog. Russell recalled an incident where a man was refusing to let a pregnant woman get into her car. She was trying to leave the embroilment. Russell pushed his way through the crowd.

"Step away from the woman and leave her alone!"

"Why? What are you going to do? Shoot me?"

"I'm not going to tell you again. Leave the woman alone and back away from the car."

Over five-hundred onlookers surrounded Deputy Russell. They were watching to see how the lone cop would handle the man. Would the lawman back away and melt into the crowd? Draw his revolver and call for help? Or would fear and adrenalin cause him to snap and start shooting into the crowd? It was a tense moment.

"What are you going to do, you big dumb hillbilly fu..." Russell released his dog. The dog jumped at the man and tore into his leg like it was playing with a rubber chew toy. The big-mouthed drunk released the woman and screamed, "*Get him off me! Get him off me! I quit!*"

After that, the rioters backed away and gave room to the deputy and his canine companion. Russell continued to walk through the crowd alone. In the background, he could hear the sirens of more police cars arriving from out of the Ozark mountains.

When the call went out, at least 125 officers responded to the riot. They were armed with mace, batons, dogs, and shotguns.

In the early morning hours of July, 1965, officers began arresting rioters. If the disruptor resisted, they used force. Even if that meant derailing a troublemaker with a flashlight or baton.

AMBUSH...

As Buff entered one cabin on the hill to confiscate liquor, his

---

[68]Russell and his brother Wandal were particularly helpful to the writer during the writing of this book.

[69]dog started barking at one of the bedroom doors. Someone or something was in there, and the dog sensed danger.

"*Come out of there!*" hollered the lawman. But there was no sound, and no one came out. The lawman gave the door a powerful kick, the door flew open, and the lawman went in. In the middle of the room, he found a man holding a chain with a large crescent wrench attached. The man had intended to ambush Buff when he walked through the door.

A few seconds later, deputies outside the bedroom heard a thud. They rushed in, picked the man up off the floor, and arrested him. "We got him, Buff!" said the lawmen as they rushed past the sheriff.

When the jail was filled, the rioters were loaded into paneled cattle trucks. From there, they were hauled to the Forsyth jail six miles away. When that jail was full, Sheriff Cardwell constructed a rope pen on the town square to corral the rioters. A couple of armed guards stood outside the rope to prevent escapes.

The next day, July 5th, Wilma Cantrell, a waitress at the Dinner Bell Cafe in Forsyth, had the misfortune of taking food to the prisoners in the jail and courtyard. She was amazed at how many people were in the courtyard and jail. It must have looked like they had arrested the whole town of Rockaway Beach.

When the riot ended, they had arrested 200 youths. Of that 200, 184 were found guilty of various misdemeanor crimes against the town. They had their night of mayhem. Now it was over.

Over two-hundred motorcycles and a thousand cars had entered the tiny resort of Rockaway Beach, Missouri, and in their wake, left property owners and city leaders with an amassment of destruction and malicious property damage. It would take weeks, if not months, to clean up and restore the town to a reasonable version of its former self.

Like a horde of locusts, visitors had entered Rockaway Beach and destroyed everything in their path. Deputy Russell Heatherly, who surveyed the town after the mob violence had this to say, "The

---

[69] Buff said the dog had saved his life.

one-room cabins looked like hog pens afterward! They destroyed the furniture in the cabins, and there were beer cans and whiskey bottles all over the place. It was hard to see it like that."

On a lighter side, driving back to Ozark the next morning with Sheriff Lamb, Ozark Police Chief Speaks heard a loud POP! A few minutes later, he smelled something strange.

"You smell that, Buff?"

"No, what?"

"Something smells funny. Like maybe it's burning. Stop the car and let's look in the trunk!"

The two opened the patrol car's trunk and discovered that a gas grenade had exploded. Coughing, Buff picked up the grenade and threw it alongside the road. The two coughed all the way back to Ozark.

THE AFTERMATH

The following night Buff did not return to Rockaway and stayed in Ozark. Lawman Christopher Donner (not his actual name) stated, "The Highway Patrol said they wouldn't come back if Buff was there. Sheriff Cardwell of Taney County told everyone that he'd take care of it." According to Donner, his (Buff's) methods of law enforcement were a little too severe. But if that meant he didn't put up with any bull, they were 100% correct.

That night, there were almost as many lawmen as there were visitors in Rockaway. They destroyed nine businesses, including the liquor store, which was completely looted. They also tore up the dancehall roof, and ripped apart countless cars. A few people had been hit with birdshot from a shotgun, but everyone survived.

The city closed three taverns because of the rioting. At least one boy was given a jail sentence for an escape from the Forsyth jail. The young man alleged that a "fat boy" who couldn't fit through a jail window, dared him to crawl through it and escape—so he did, but was quickly apprehended.

Rockaway Beach, Missouri never recovered as a family vacation resort. Fifty-two years later, the little berg has all but dried up. But in its heyday, the 1920s-1965, it was known as one of America's favorite vacation spots.

Back in Ozark, Buff couldn't care less if he returned to

Rockaway Beach. He had bigger fish to fry back home. Buff was working on his first bank robbery case.

The armed bank robber entered the Nixa Bank lobby wearing dark sunglasses, a plaid shirt, straw hat, and a white bandage over his nose and upper lip. In less than five minutes he had absconded with over $6,000 in cash from the bank.

Buff notified the FBI and Highway Patrol while he and his deputies set up roadblocks all over the county. The man who had stuck a gun in [70]W.F. Coffman's stomach during the robbery, was never captured. And to my knowledge, the money was never recovered either.

Sheriff Lamb had no way of knowing it, but that July, he was about to make a move that would put the entire town behind him and launch him into legendary status. Even the people he stopped as a town marshal in the 1950s had to admit that Sheriff Lamb was now a roaring lion… wearing a badge.

---

[70] Coffman was in the bank that day to do business. Coffman died at 87 in 1976.

CHAPTER ELEVEN

PROTECTING OZARK

The sun beat down on the streets of Ozark, with temperatures reaching into the 90s by noon. Buff had just walked into his office when the dispatcher hollered at him.

"Sheriff, you have a phone call. You'd better pick up. It sounds urgent!"

"Lamb here! When? How many do you think? I'll take care of it. Thanks." (Click). Buff stepped into the dispatcher's room.

"Call Russell, Bill (Lawrence), Jim (Casey), and Ray (Speak) and tell them to meet me out on the courthouse lawn."

The sheriff had received word that a group of bikers was headed south towards Ozark. After what he, Russell Heatherly, and Chief of Police Ray Speak had seen in [71]Rockaway Beach, Buff was not going to allow the bikers to pass through Ozark!

PROTECT THE TOWN...

Buff looked over at one of his deputies. "Roust anyone you can in town and tell them to grab whatever they can and meet me down at the Finley bridge. These SOB's aren't going to treat my town

---

[71]Over 200 motorcycles had ridden into Rockaway.

like they did Rockaway!"

It was a classic western setting. A group of wild cattle rovers, riding into town to raise some Hell. They needed to be stopped. The sheriff could hightail it out of town on business, or he could stand up to the alleged outlaws, some of whom might be armed. Sheriff Buff Lamb did something even bigger.

As a group of 12-15 motorcycles neared Ozark, people congregated on the bridge leading into town, near NN highway. They were armed with rakes, baseball bats, and even a frying pan. Volunteer firefighter, Bill Hanks, had hooked a fire hose to a hydrant to repel the bikers in case they made it past Buff. But that wasn't going to happen.

Evelyn Gentile recalled the following: "I remember seeing several men gathered around the courthouse that day. At least one of them had a baseball bat."

"You folks back up on the curve by the Dairy Queen. My deputies and I will stop them on the bridge," shouted the Sheriff. Standing beside Buff were Russell Heatherly and Ray Speak. In 2015, I spoke to both men, and this is what they saw and heard.

"We went around town asking people to help, and they dropped what they were doing to defend Ozark. People may say they didn't like Buff, but they sure helped him defend the town that day!" said Russell Heatherly.

"When the Bikers arrived, Buff stood in the middle of the road and told them to turn around. I know you boys are headed to Branson, but they've had a lot of trouble down there, and they don't need anymore! So, turn them bikes around and go somewhere else."

"They revved up their motorcycles and started to leave, but the leader then turned and came back. They weren't wearing any jacket's but a few of them had vests. I didn't know if they were Hells Angels or who. When the guy tried to rev his bike and turn in close to Buff, Buff knocked him off the bike with a club! A couple more of them turned around and Buff hollered, *"Get him Ray!"* So I swung the pine club Buff had given me and knocked the man off his motorcycle and broke his taillight!" recalled former Chief of Police, Ray Speak.

"They would come up and try to make a U-turn on the bridge to show off, and Buff would thump one with his stick. I even thumped one or two! They were all dirty and a rough bunch!"—Russell Heatherly

"After the motorcycles left, a man drove up and said a man had been hit by a car and was lying in the ditch. A car had not hit that man! He lost control of his motorcycle and fell off it!" said Ray Speak.

Stan Shelton a long-time friend of Buff's was there that day.

"A motorcycle group had come to see what was going on down in Rockaway Beach. Troop D (Highway Patrol) had told Buff they didn't want any more people coming there looking around. One boy, on a Honda 90, tried to go pass Buff, and Buff flipped him right off the bike! Now after that, we were kind of told to break up the people on the hill that were watching and go about our business". —Stan Shelton. A long-time friend of Buff's. He was there that day.

The citizens of Ozark had turned the Biker Gang around. The town felt proud of itself. Locals had watched their town Sheriff and his deputies stop a gang of dirty, threatening [72]bikers. Sheriff Lamb did what he promised to do; he had protected his town and county.

Word of the incident propelled Sheriff Buff Lamb into a vortex of legendary status. The former cowboy, daredevil, and town marshal was now a folklore legend. But it didn't stop there.

After the riot in Rockaway Beach and the incident on the Finley River Bridge, a rumor surfaced. The Missouri Highway Patrol had received information. At least two hundred motorcycles planned to return to Rockaway Beach on Labor Day weekend for retribution.

According to Buff Lamb, he received a call Saturday, September 4th. The gang was coming to Ozark to "ride the streets out". For ten days, he had received such warnings. The motorcycle gang was coming to terrorize Ozark and its inhabitants. He didn't have a minute to lose.

Ozark was in danger. Maybe standing up to a motorcycle gang was not such a good idea after all. Not if it meant gaining their wrath and fury for revenge.

---

[72] Some people said it was the Hells Angels Buff turned around that day. I heard the same rumor as a kid, but there is no proof of it. A lot of folks believe it was just a motorcycle club.

"They (Highway Patrol) wanted me in Rockaway Beach, but I sent my deputies there instead. I stayed here (Ozark) in case something happened," stated Sheriff Lamb.

"Sure enough, sixty to ninety minutes after I got a phone call that a gang was headed here, I spotted them coming into Ozark on Missouri 14, the US 65 cutoff into town."

Buff claimed he passed some bikers (sixteen) from behind and cut them off. Buff got in front of the bikers and blocked the road. "That many more, came up behind me!" said the sheriff.

The hard-boiled lawman met the youths about eighty yards in front of the bridge leading into town. Sheriff Lamb was surrounded by revving engines and squalling tires. But the Sheriff maintained his composure, just as he had a few months before.

"You boys *go back to where you came from!*" he exclaimed above the roar of the motorcycle engines! One boy yelled back, "*We don't have to!*" Two men on motorcycles drove past the Sheriff. And that, according to Sheriff Buff Lamb, was when the "head knockin'" took place.

It is said there is a thin line between bravery and stupidity. Buff walked the line that day. He was one sheriff against over thirty motorcycles. But he was there, and it was time to act.

Buff began kicking bikes and [73]swinging his oak club at bikers while they taunted and attempted to usurp his authority. [74]Dirty Harry would have been proud!

"Either you boys turn around, or I'll put every one of you in jail!"

The gang revved up their cycles to drown out the sheriffs' commands, but they did turn their bikes around and headed north out of Ozark. Sheriff Lamb successfully turned another motorcycle gang around, which further proved he was as tough as people said he was.

Placing his shotgun back in the rack in his office, Buff immediately summoned his deputies back to Ozark from Rockaway. Later that night, the sister of one boy in the earlier group of thwarted bikers, returned to Ozark and threatened the

---

[73]Four of the boys later tried to get Buff to pay for their hospital bills. Buff never paid a dime.

[74] Fictious Client Eastwood character.

Sheriff.

"I promise, and guarantee you, that there will be over two-hundred motorcycles down here, and there will be *serious trouble!*"

"I wouldn't do that, Missy, because I will lock every one of them, and you, in my jail!" The woman left, and the Sheriff called in his deputies.

"Men, I want you to round up some boys and I want every entrance and exit into this town sewed up! If they come back, we're putting them all in jail! Now *get out there!*" The town had no way of knowing it, but Buff had just declared martial law.

Nothing happened over the next few days except for a few threats. A couple of lowlifes called his home and threatened him and his family, but none of them made good on it. Someone even called in a bomb threat to get back at the Sheriff. The bikers, however, never returned to Ozark.

The story of Sheriff Lamb and the [75]"Hells Angels Gang" spread throughout Missouri, and states beyond. He was ascribed as one of the toughest lawmen in the state. A sheriff akin to old-time western lawmen like Wild Bill Hickok and Wyatt Earp.

Buff was not the kind of Sheriff who hid behind the badge. [76]John Nix recalled an incident when he was a small boy in Ozark.

"My uncle and two old-timers were at Junior Cooks' filling station when a fellow drove up and said that a man named William Gold was meeting Buff across the street in the church parking lot. Gold had phoned Buff and told him to meet him because he was going to kick his ass. A few minutes later, Buff arrived alone, and sat in the parking lot waiting for Gold, who never showed. Buff sat there for about twenty minutes, then left."

July 1965 ended with an incident at a Pentecostal Church in neighboring town of Spokane. During their Revival, a guitar player

---

[75] They were not the Hells Angels. The motorcyclists were from Springfield. But the Hells Angels Gang made better coffee shop gossip.

[76] Real name withheld.

stepped outside, spotted a copperhead snake, and killed it. Before the revival ended two nights later, 93 poisonous snakes had been killed at the church. The vibration of the music had drawn the snakes in from the surrounding brush.

In August 1965 Buff received information that two men from Kansas City had been seen stealing a yacht from Kimberling City on Table Rock Lake. Buff gathered up deputy J.B. Casey and waited for the men in case they came toward Ozark.

Sure enough, the car towing the boat cruiser came up the road toward them at 11:20 pm. Buff and J. B. arrested the two and took them to jail. One of them had a badge and [77]deputy commission from another town. That did not deter the lawmen from doing their job.

Buff Next to Patrol Car

---

[77] The case was dismissed. The deputy commission badge returned to Jackson County, Mo.

Chapter Twelve

TROUBLE IN THE JAIL

The town of Chadwick announced their annual snake hunt. A church near Chadwick told newspapers they would not cancel their Revival, even though they had killed three-hundred deadly poisonous copperhead snakes near the church.

October 27th, 1967, Buff received information that some boys were scheming to set some hay bales on fire that were stacked at a construction site near Nixa. The next day, a Sunday, Sheriff Lamb sat atop a mountain of straw and waited for the arsonist to appear. Buff checked the time, midnight, one and 2:00am passed when Buff heard three boys approaching, talking in whispers.

"Let's take a breather before we set it because we'll have to run back to the car," said one boy.

The young men spoke in hushed voices oblivious that Buff was 10 feet above them, hidden in the hay. Suddenly, the Sheriff arose like a ghost from the grave and shouted, *"Don't move boys! You're all under arrest!"*

The boys froze, then turned and bolted. Sheriff Lamb climbed down from the hay bales and [78]fired his revolver into the air. "I said, *don't move!*"

---

[78] Straight out of a Hopalong Cassidy movie.

Eighteen-year-old [79]Daniel Allen Hicks immediately stopped. He may have recognized Sheriff Lamb and thought the next shot would be in his back. When Sheriff Lamb told you to do something, you did it! The word was out, Lamb was one mean son-of-a-bitch.

Buff took Hicks back to the boys' car and took the car keys from the ignition. "Now you stand there, boy, while I call for help." "Christian County 101 to Christian County 109!"

"Go ahead, Sheriff!"

"Ray, I need some help to round up some boys here in Nixa!"

"No problem Sheriff. Help is on the way."

Later that morning, deputies captured Jack Martin and [80]Robert C. Knauer and took them to jail as well.

Three months later, 42-year-old Buff Lamb was back in the hospital with a knee injury he had suffered in a car accident. He spent several days in Springfield Baptist Hospital before being released.

In 1966, Sheriff Lamb arrested a man who thought he didn't have to follow the sheriff's orders. He thought wrong. When he became threatening and belligerent, Buff busted a nightstick over his head. That's the way things were handled in the old days. Wyatt Earp would have used a pistol; Buff used a nightstick. This wasn't 1876, it was 1967. And Buff wasn't in Wichita, he was in Ozark, Missouri.

It was Deputy Heatherly's job to escort the prisoner to the Missouri State Penitentiary. Along the way, Russell stopped the car to let the man use the restroom. Once inside, the prisoner locked the door and refused to come out. Russell had two choices, bust down the door or wait him out. Waiting him out was not an option. Russell called Buff back at Ozark.

"Buff, this guy has locked himself in the restroom and won't come out."

"That son of a… *kick down the door and mace him real good!*"

That was Buff's answer to everything. If a prisoner didn't comply, then use force, and don't be nice about it! The law had to

---

[79]Daniel Allen Hicks became a successful individual. The hay bale incident was a prank.

[80] Robert Knauer lived a successful and crime-free life.

be obeyed, and Buff expected his deputies to be just as tough as he was. The prisoner ended up going with Deputy Heatherly. His barricade plan had failed.

A summer night in 1967 Larry Bennett (name withheld) and some friends were cruising Ozark looking for girls, as kids often did. The driver of the teenage foursome was from Christian County.

While Larry sat in the backseat sipping beer from a can, a Christian County star packer pulled the boys over. A big man with a flashlight stepped over to the car. It was Sheriff Buff Lamb.

"What're you boys doing in Ozark tonight?"

The driver spoke up.

"Nothing Sheriff, just cruising the square." The sheriff shined his flashlight in Larry's face. Larry was in the back seat behind the driver.

"What's your name, boy?"

"Who the fu... wants to know?"

The next thing [81]Larry remembered was being pulled through the car's back window. No one spoke to Sheriff Lamb that way. Nobody! Especially a punk kid in his town!

"The next thing I remember was a one-arm kid who knew Buff rushing over to him. He told Buff that he knew us and that we were okay. If that kid hadn't stopped Buff, I don't know what would have happened. Buff stuffed me back in the car and told us to "Git!" We left and never came back to Ozark."

Inside the jail, unhappy with Buff's hotel, prisoners stopped up their toilets and flooded the place. That would teach the big-shot sheriff! Now they would get better treatment. But the jailbirds didn't know who they were messing with.

Evelynn Gentile and her husband Charles, went down to help Buff. This is what they recalled: "Buff took 'em by the hairs of their head, stuck their heads in the toilets, and flushed it. Now, do it again (flood)! And he made them help clean it up." If you were a guest at Buff's hotel, you did not want management coming down on you. Several residents found that out the hard way.

Down at Lindenlure, five men from Springfield approached

---

[81] Larry grew up and retired from the Springfield Police Department as a Detective. I worked with him after he retired.

Frankie Walker. The gang ordered him to surrender his wallet. When Walker refused, they broke out his car window. But that didn't work either.

George Oliver Bressie, George Metts, and Roscoe Choate Jr then attacked Walker, beating him with their fists and belts.

The five escaped with $14, a watch, and a spotlight. Sheriff Lamb quickly captured the men and jailed them. The next day, July 4th, 1969, Buff walked into the Sheriff's office.

"Are you sure you want me to go home, Sheriff?" said the night dispatcher.

"Sure, you boys have a family. Luella can dispatch, and I'll feed the prisoners."

"They were quiet last night, but those boys seem a little mean."

"They're just boys. Get on out of here and get some sleep before the parade."

"Okay, thanks Sheriff."

Buff fed his prisoners scrambled eggs, toast, and two pieces of bacon and went back for coffee. When he returned, the boys were whispering.

"What's going on in there?" No answer, so the Sheriff unlocked the door and walked into the large cell.

Prisoner George Bressie, stepped in front of Buff. He was six-foot-tall and 170 pounds. The Sheriff could see the men had been working on tearing out the cell windows.

"Who broke out these windows?"

Bressie was the spokesman for the men. "I don't know nothing about any windows!" With that said, Bressie attempted to sucker punch the courthouse lawman.

Buff stepped to his right and slugged the unruly convict, knocking him to the floor. The other two prisoners started for Lamb, but he rapidly locked the cell door behind him and darted up the corridor to his office and called Luella at home.

"I need the Highway Patrol and my deputies! The prisoners have busted out some windows and are attempting to escape!"

A few minutes later, a Highway Patrolman arrived with one of Buff's deputies. The lawmen secured the prisoners in their cells. One or two of the prisoners may have accidentally fallen down a time or two. It happens to unruly, fractious thugs.

After Buff completed his report, George Bressie received

counseling on the dangers of escaping from custody, and the problems associated with striking the County Sheriff. It was a "private" counseling intervention between Buff and Bressie.

With the prisoners all nestled in their cells, life continued in Ozark, Missouri. The robbery charges against Bressie for assaulting and robbing Walker were later dropped. The victim (Walker) refused to testify against the boys. A huge mistake.

[82]George Oliver Bressie was later charged with stealing, theft, burglary, and escape. He was a rotten apple, and it would take a long time for him to change his ways. But one thing was for certain, he'd never forget Sheriff Buff Lamb.

After fights, escapes, motorcycle gangs, and a riot, you'd think things would calm down. But they didn't.

While on patrol, Police Chief [83]Ray Speak, observed a man robbing the Skelly Service Station. From inside the station, the man fired a shotgun at Ray, splattering buckshot all over his patrol car. Ray survived the murder attempt, and the burglar was captured a few days later.

In May 1968, eight men filed for Christian County Sheriff: Pletcher Rogers, [84]Delbert Weter, Joe Mayberry, Elmer Martin, Bill Lawrence, James R. Allen, Luther Meadows, former sheriff Jack Monger and Sheriff Buff Lamb.

A few days before the Republican Primary, Buff arrested three men. The arrest helped clear up six burglaries. Sheriff Lamb and his men were vigilant when apprehending criminals. Buff expected the best from his deputies, and he got it, because they respected him.

Buff won the primary for Sheriff. Joe Mayberry was second. Jack Monger was third. And [85]Pletcher Rogers fell to the bottom of the pack beating Jim Allen. The county had spoken—they wanted Buff Lamb as their Sheriff.

In other parts of Southern Missouri, [86]Eugene Fraker beat Oral

---

[82] George Oliver Bressie continued his life of crime. But he stayed out of Christian County, Missouri.
[83] In 1969 they bumped Ray's pay up to $17.50 a week.
[84] Delbert owned a garage in Ozark.
[85] Pletcher stated in 2017; "I only ran because the people wanted me to. I spent less than $300 on my campaign".
[86] This writer received a Deputy Commission from Eugene Fraker.

Davidson in Webster County. In Taney County, Lyman Cardwell beat Carl Wallace. In Stone County, Richard Barnes beat Kenneth Holt.

Thirty-three guns were stolen from the V&S Hardware store in Ozark at the Highway shopping center. Enough guns to take over the town. They never recovered the guns. Hopefully, they wouldn't be used in Ozark.

On August 27th, 1968, Sheriff Lamb searched for and found a fifteen-year-old boy who had drowned in the James River outside of Nixa. Walking along the banks of the popular fishing spot, he found the child's body still in the water. The boy had dived in after his fishing pole and was swept away by the current.

A tough man with lawbreakers, Buff cried later that day after carrying the boy's wet body to his car. It was a side of Buff no one had seen except his ex-wives. Speaking of ex-wives, the marriage between Luella and Buff had lasted about 6 years before ending.

"I knew Buff and Luella, been to their house many times. I knew Luella well. The things she told me about Buff! I didn't like the man. He had a split personality. He could be nice, but also mean! Buff was the type to love them, leave them, and then take everything they had. Buff broke Luella's heart and took her money. He wanted her to sell her house and give him the money. He said he'd pay her back, but he never did." --[87]Darlene Weller 2016

Four days after finding the drowned boy, Buff married [88]Clara Alice (Anderson) Moore. Clara was Buff's sixth wife. Buff was Clara's second husband. Her ex-husband, Charles Franklin Moore, passed away less than a year before.

---

[87]Darlene Weller—a fictitious name used to hide the person's real identity. This source knew Mary Lee as well and stated that Mary Lee had grieved over losing Buff.

[88]Throughout this writer's research, not one person spoke ill of Clara. Everyone who met her loved her. Deputies I spoke to said she was friendly, generous, and a superb cook. Clara dispatched for Buff, fed his prisoners, and rode with him on patrol. After having spoken to Clara myself, I could see why she was so well-liked. She is kind, articulate, helpful, and has an outstanding personality.

The next month, Buff investigated a complaint of bullets in a man's boat. After a few days, the sheriff arrested the man responsible for the damage. Few crimes during Buff's administration went unsolved, but that would soon change.

Sheriff L.E. Lamb was about to become involved in a missing woman case that would tear the community apart. The case still lingers in the minds of many of its citizens. The Christian County Hero was about to take a tumble.

Bressie, Hensley and Choate Jr.

CHAPTER THIRTEEN

MURDER, THREATS AND SUSPICION

Twenty-year-old, Neva Carol (Horton) Blades, disappeared from a laundromat in Nixa on December 15th, 1969. Later that day, her car was found parked on Highway 160. Her husband, Larry, immediately called the Sheriff's office.

When Sheriff Lamb heard the news, he was target shooting at an underground firing range, in the basement of the Campbell Ford Garage in Ozark.

"Russell, get over there and see what's going on. Take [89]Bill (McNabb) with you!"

When the two arrived at the scene, they were shocked by what they saw. In the time it had taken them to drive 10 miles from Ozark to Nixa, bystanders had ransacked the Blades car.

"The doors and trunk were open, even the hood of the car was open! Curious onlookers had been inside the car and touched everything. Even the radiator cap!" said former reserve deputy Russell Heatherly.

Using sarcasm, the deputy stated, "I appreciate you guys touching everything!" Retrieving any fingerprints was now impossible.

---

[89] Bill McNabb was a Reserve Deputy and the current Fire Chief. He also drove a school bus, and he had his own Automotive Business.

In the book, *A Body on A Farm*, by [90]Barbara Kemm-Highton, it's reported that the car sat for over 48 hours before being towed. Deputy Heatherly remembered calling a tow truck the same day he investigated the missing woman.

The day after Mrs. Blades came up missing, people from all over the county turned out to search for her, including the Red Cross, who handed out drinks and sandwiches.

A former Christian County Deputy remembered, "I thought it was strange that Carol's husband, did not join the search."

Larry Blades, [91]Carol's husband, even became a suspect. After all, he was allegedly sleeping at his house alone when he received the news. In some people's opinions, Larry had acted peculiar about the whole incident.

For the next few weeks, Buff and his deputies searched everywhere for Carol Blades. And they interviewed possible suspects. The clues led nowhere. Had she taken off and left her husband, or was something more sinister at play? There were lots of questions, but no answers.

Said one deputy, "We didn't sleep, eat, or spend time with our families. Finding Mrs. Blades was a priority for us. I recall sleeping while another deputy drove. When he got tired, we'd switch places, but we never gave up on finding that woman. Clara, Buff's wife, always had food ready for us since we spent such long hours searching for the missing woman."

Deputies learned that Mrs. Blades was wearing a white coat the day of her disappearance. "I remember we saw something white way out in a field, so we stopped the car and walked a long way to see what it was. It turned out; it was a white goat. We did everything we could to find that woman!" said deputy Russell Heatherly.

---

[90]To my knowledge, they never interviewed Russell for Mrs. Kemm-Highton's book.

[91] The two married on June 16, 1967. Carol was 17 and Larry was 20.

RUMORS BEGAN TO FLY…

Then an ugly rumor spread about the Sheriff. A rumor that the sheriff had killed Mrs. Blades and buried her under some cement. Everyone knew what a womanizer Buff was. It was no secret. Women were something to conquer and throw away when you were finished with them. Buff was the type to have an affair with a young married woman.

Unfounded, it was later discovered that the rumor had come from the mind of a disgruntled enemy of Buff. People were looking for someone to blame, and Buff was at the top of the list.

[92]Allegedly, Buff's wife Clara remembered Buff coming home with blood on his shirt. About the time of Blades's disappearance. In 2015 this writer spoke to Buff's former wife [93]Clara, about the rumor.

"I never heard that one," said the former Mrs. Lamb. "No, nothing like that ever happened!"

"Did anyone from Mrs. Kemm-Highton's book ever contact you about the Blades disappearance?".

"No, they did not."

So, this writer contacted several deputies, and people who knew Buff at the time. A few laughed at the absurdity that Buff might have been involved in the disappearance. The rest recalled that Sheriff Lamb had been at the firing range with his deputies and firearms trainers.

"Buff made too many trips to Jefferson City looking for that woman to have had anything to do with it," said former Buff Lamb's friend, Stan Shelton, in 2017.

The missing woman's family pressured the Sheriff's department to find their daughter, especially now she had now been gone for months. One woman interviewed, recalled a family member sitting outside the sheriff's office for hours. Staring at Sheriff Lamb, she wanted answers to Carol's disappearance.

A few months into the investigation, Sheriff Lamb got fed up with the family "[94]harassment". Buff even forbade Chief of Police

---

[92] From the book A Body on A Farm by Mrs. Kemm-Heighton.

[93] Wife Clara stated that she had not been interviewed for any books, nor had she made any statements about Buff.

[94] If you could call it harassment. They simply wanted answers.

Ray Speak from talking to that "old man", (Carol Blades father) as he called him.

"You can't tell me who to talk to and not to talk to, Buff!"

"I'm telling you Ray, *quit talking to them!*"

"I'll talk to who *I want!* I don't work for you, Buff!"

"Buff believed he could control me, but he couldn't!" said Speaks.

Had Carol Blades run away, left with another man, or had she been kidnapped? Or worse yet, had she been murdered? There was nothing to indicate where she had gone, or what had happened to her. Investigators quickly came to a complete blank on her disappearance. In the courthouse, Sheriff Lamb felt the outrage of not solving the case of the missing homemaker.

"It might have been some people she knew in Ava," speculated Mr. Shelton.

In October of 1970, Larry Blades told the Springfield Leader and Press that he and Carol went out on a date on October 15, 1967. Maybe he forgot the couple married on June 16, 1967? Or the paper got it wrong?

The search for Carol Blades continued for the next year, and it looked like her body would never be found. There were too many hills, hollers, and caves to make a person disappear in—if that's what you wanted to do. Then there was a break in the case.

While looking for his cattle on his farm on Christmas day, 1970, around two in the afternoon, seventy-three-year-old, [95]Ernest (Ernie) Wilhelm came across a skeleton in a stand of cedar trees.

Normally the old farmer would have dismissed the skull since he said he had found several Indian skulls on his land. But this time was different. He also observed scattered bones and a pair of purple pants.

Ernie rushed home and told his family about the find. He called Richard Barnes, the Stone County Sheriff. Clara, Buff's wife, was working as a dispatcher that day. She recalled the Stone County Sheriff brought the remains of the body to Ozark in a trash bag. Clara immediately dispatched the Sheriff. Meanwhile, Sheriff Barnes took the remains to Harris Funeral Home in Ozark.

Chief of Police Ray Speak recalled that day. "Sheriff Barnes

---

[95] Ernest Wilhelm passed away on November 10, 1979, at the age of 82.

came to me and asked, "Where is the Sheriff?"

"He's at home."

"Call him and tell him to get out here and you watch the expression on Buff's face when he sees what I have in the trunk of my car."

A few minutes later, Buff arrived.

"Look in the trunk, Buff!" said Sheriff Barnes. Buff got the keys out of the ignition and popped open the trunk. Chief of Police Ray Speak said standing next to him, "Buff's face turned white." It was Carol Blades body.

THE MISSING WOMAN FOUND...

Christmas morning 1970 Sheriff Lamb drove to Stone County. An hour later, he and Sheriff Barnes started their investigation. Once considered a suspect, Buff walked the area looking for clues of what might have happened.

Clara Lamb recalled bringing sandwiches and cookies to the men who searched the area. People interested in the case swiftly converged on the crime scene.

"I couldn't believe that they were letting people walk around the crime scene!" said Mrs. Lamb. One former Highway Patrolman recalled; "It looked like [96]Buff was trying to destroy the evidence the way he walked around kicking leaves and brush."

A few days later, deputy Gene Haworth took a metal detector down to the area. Strewn about, he found a couple of rings belonging to the missing woman. Without a doubt, they had found the body of Mrs. Carol Blades.

Two days passed when Sheriff James (Richard) Barnes was quoted in newspapers. "We found no signs of foul play." In other words, they found no evidence of broken bones or trauma to the woman's skull.

Meanwhile, back in Ozark, a serious rift emerged between the Chief of Police Ray Speak and Sheriff Lamb. It began when a young woman came to Ray while he was on duty sitting in his

---

[96] By now, Buff had attended Sheriff's training. He knew about preserving evidence at a crime scene.

patrol car. She was crying.

She told Ray that Buff Lamb had pulled her over, and "accosted" her during the stop. To get away from the sheriff, she stated she had kicked the sheriff's injured legs.

"Go home and tell your husband!" said the Police Chief.

"No, if I do, he will kill Buff!"

"Then go back home and I'll take care of this."

When Ray got off duty that morning, he went up to the sheriff's office. He had to know for himself. Had Buff said and did what the woman alleged? Had he really tried to force himself on the young woman? She definitely seemed frightened and emotionally traumatized. Deputy Bill McNabb was in the office.

"Morning, Bill!"

"Morning, Ray!"

"Hey, is the sheriff in? I need to talk to him?"

"No, he's running late but I will call him at home."

"Thanks."

Looking out the window, the sun was peeping over the buildings on the town square. Ray looked down and saw Buff pull into zone one (Sheriff's parking). Maybe the whole sexual assault thing was a big misunderstanding.

Buff got out of his patrol car and the first thing Ray noticed was that Buff was limping worse than usual. His legs had been tormenting him something awful lately, but this morning it was unusually bad. The sheriff came upstairs and walked into another office. Ray remembered it was a room where they listened to phone calls. When he exited, Ray followed him and noticed that the sheriff had his leg propped up on a desk and was rubbing his knee.

"What's the matter, Buff?"

"Oh, my leg is bothering me today." Just those words were more than Ray could take! He was sure the young girl was telling the truth! The young woman [97]claimed that Buff propositioned her and that she had to kick his legs to get away from him. Next, Buff walked into the sheriff's office still complaining about his legs hurting. It was too much of a coincidence to ignore.

---

[97] This was not the first, second, or even third time a woman had complained that the sheriff intimidated or tried to force himself on them.

"I hope it rots, you son-of-a-bitch!" Then I walked out, Ray said.

Buff was a good man and a good sheriff, but he *could not* leave the women alone. And he used his position as a county official to stop, harass and meet young women. He wasn't the first or last law enforcement officer to do this, but he was scaring women in town. Buff didn't care if you were single or married, only that you were young, pretty, and under his control.

BUFF IS GOING TO KILL ME...

After that incident and a few others, [98]Ray believed Buff might try to kill him. You did NOT want to be on Buff's nasty side. Buff cast a long shadow in Ozark and Christian County. In fact, his reputation as a hard-nosed, tough lawman had far exceeded Missouri's southern counties. Those who had crossed him, described Buff as "mean and ruthless".

Ozark had a sheriff who liked to hunt. He hunted bears, moose, elk, deer, he didn't care about the size of an animal. What mattered was dispatching a bullet to their heart or lungs. A shot that would put your prey down in a pool of blood with quick and pinpoint accuracy.

If you were in Buff's way, and he wanted rid of you, he had the position, ability, and means to make it happen. However, if he liked you, he could be as gentle as a one-day-old kitten. But if you made that kitten mad, or he considered you an enemy, that kitten became a wounded grizzly bear. We all have it in us to turn mean, if necessary, Buff just didn't need as much prodding as the rest of us to bring out the monster.

After defying Buff a few times, the heat was on. The longer Buff chewed on a bone, the sharper his teeth got. Buff was re-evaluating who his friends were, and were not. The Carol Blades case had Buff untying knots everywhere he went. A lot of people suspected Buff of foul play and rumors were spreading. Then there was Chief of Police, Ray Speak, sticking his nose in things. It

---

[98] Ray Speak was not afraid of Buff, but he knew how dangerous he could be if crossed. And Ray was on Buff's bad side.

seemed like Ray wasn't the close friend Buff thought he was. Ray's involvement in Buff's business needed to be stopped.

Sitting in his patrol car, Ray ran a string of scenarios in his mind. What would he do if Buff came after him? Ray knew a lot about Buff, but more importantly, he knew what Buff was capable of. Buff knew a lot about Ray. Where he ate, slept, when he went on patrol, and his personal habits. If Buff wanted to hurt Ray, he could set him up. Ray had to do something. Ray's scent was in the wind, and it was possible the hunter was moving in on him.

After much deliberation on Ray's part while sitting in his patrol car on duty, he decided to draft a letter. He had to choose his wording correctly, and make sure it fell into the proper hands.

"If anything happens to me, I want you to give this to the prosecutor's office," he told a friend. The letter named Buff Lamb as the number one suspect in his death. He suspected that Buff might try to kill him.

Ray's interview:

This writer: "Ray, did you really believe Buff might try to kill you?"

Ray: "Oh yes, I believed he was going to kill me! He hated me! I started sitting in my car with a pistol on my lap."

Chief of Police Ray Speak was no pushover. What he lacked in height, he made up for in heart. When he wasn't enforcing the law in Ozark, he was winning motorcycle races and working as a stock car builder and mechanic.

The weeks passed, and the threat of Buff shooting or harming Ray lessened. But Ray stayed alert. Buff was not to be trifled with. From what Ray knew about Buff, having worked and ridden with him, he'd have no trouble getting rid of a problem, "permanently".

The death of the young woman was working on the minds of the entire county. A young girl had been killed, and the murderer was still at large. Tempers flared, and rumors spread through Christian County like a fire with the wind at its back.

Some people believed Sheriff Lamb had knowledge of the murder. Others believed he was incapable of such a heinous crime. If Buff was not guilty, there were times he made himself look quite suspicious.

Time passed, and Clara, Buff's wife, volunteered to take a polygraph test. The highway patrol saw no reason for it, so she didn't. To this writer's knowledge, Buff never took a polygraph test, but why should he? There was no evidence linking him to the woman's disappearance. It was alleged that Carol Blades' husband, Larry, took a lie detector test twice, but nothing linked him to the disappearance. Suspect after suspect was brought in, but no one was charged.

The investigation waned. To this day, over forty-five years later, the murderer of Neva Carol Blades has never been found. He may have even passed away by now.

One former deputy told me three calls were received from a man claiming he had "proof" that Buff was a dirty sheriff, and, that he had information about the Blades murder pointing to Buff. Three times, Sheriff's deputies went to meet the mysterious stranger. They dressed in civilian clothes, and three times the man never showed. The deputies had orders to capture the man and bring him back to Buff for questioning.

Oddly in 1965 a woman in Neosho had vanished just like Carol Blades in broad daylight. They discovered her car along a road. Her body was in a thicket just like Mrs. Blades. Her abductor was never captured either. Maybe the two deaths were connected—no one knows.

During interviews for this book, a man told me J. M. (real name withheld) lived by the laundry and was related to Buff. He also got his gravel close to where Carol Blades' body was found. According to the storyteller, a woman was listening to her scanner when she heard, "He's Killing Me! He's Killing Me!" J. M. allegedly owed Buff $1,500, but after the murder, the debt was cleared.

Having spoken to a former deputy who knew Sheriff Lamb in the 1980s, I was told that anytime the Blades murder came up in conversation, Buff would turn red and get extremely mad. It was an unsolved case and a blot on his record.

Today, in 2022, the murder still goes unsolved. Buff was interviewed about the crime on many occasions. Investigators asked former wife Clara if she thought Buff was a suspect. She told the investigators that she was sure he had nothing to do with it.

It is this writer's sincere hope that the murder is [99]solved one day. Someone, somewhere, has information about what happened. The murderer may be alive or dead or they may have moved away. Or…, they may still be living in the area and are between the ages of seventy and ninety years old. Among organized crime, there's a saying "the only way two people can keep a secret, is if one of them is dead."

As for Sheriff Buff Lamb, the rumors about who killed Mrs. Blades would haunt him for the rest of his life. No matter where he went or what he did, people wanted to know about the missing woman from Nixa. And they still do.

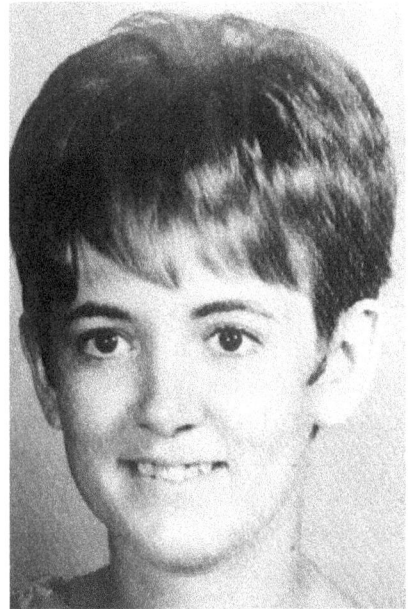

Carol Neva Blades

---

[99] In 2020, while attending a Law Enforcement seminar in Branson, Missouri, I met a Christian County Deputy. He is currently working on the Carol Blades murder.

CHAPTER FOURTEEN

THE ROCK FESTIVAL

Buff didn't like hippies, long hair, protesters, or drugs. All that flower power, give peace a chance, folk music, anti-Vietnam crap was created for a bunch of pansies. Everyone knew peace rallies, sit-ins, and pacifism bull made the cowboy sheriff nauseous. Buff was old school. He listened to country music, hated communism, peace signs, and wouldn't be caught dead in a tie-dye tee shirt. Buff believed a man should look like a man, and act like a man. Drugs and underage drinking killed people, and he wasn't about to let that get started in his county.

The hatred of our brave Vietnam soldiers made no sense to him. He was not a religious man, but he believed in '*God, Guns, and Country*'. So, when Rock Festival advertisers asked Buff if they could put on a show at the old drag strip, he flatly refused.

With festivals came drugs, alcohol, nudity, and long-haired hippies. Everything Buff detested. Rock concerts were happening all over the country. Woodstock was still fresh in everyone's mind from the year before.

That might be okay somewhere else, but not in Christian County. The concert was moved to Greene County. Outside of

Springfield on a 530-acre farm belonging to Veterinarian [100]Walter W. Love. The doctor leased 100 acres to the concert promoters. Now it was Sheriff Mickey Owens' problem.

The rules were:
Music must be kept at a reasonable volume.

There would be adequate toilet facilities. No urinating and defecating on the festival grounds.

Enough law enforcement officers to cover the event

No alcohol or drugs are sold or permitted on the farm.

No drugs of any kind.

Law enforcement may kick anyone off the property who broke the rules.

Sheriff Owens gathered his reserve deputies, the Highway Patrol, and Sheriff Buff Lamb to help. If things got out of hand, he wanted plenty of Law Enforcement on hand. Officers helped with parking and any troublemakers or drugs.

No drugs at a rock festival? Who were they kidding? This was 1970, not 1950. Of course, there would be drugs. A huge part of America's culture was into recreational drug use.

"The concert was scheduled on a Saturday. But the drugs were hidden on the farm three days before. If an attendee wanted drugs, he bought a piece of paper telling him where the stash was hidden," said a former officer.

With the concert in full swing, officers busted patrons buying and selling drugs. They arrested a few for concealing firearms, driving while intoxicated, and careless driving. They escorted one woman to jail for nudity.

Before the concert ended, they made forty arrests. Promoters estimated that 4,500 people had attended the festival.

On the day of the festival, a Friday night, deputies stopped a van. Inside were two men. The two had been drinking that day, one of the men celebrating his birthday.

The two were detained because a wreck had blocked the road.

---

[100] Mr. Love had been told it would be a "Memorial Service for Vietnam War dead". A place where he could take his 10 and 12-year-old children. Not a "rock Festival". Springfield Leader and Press September 10, 1970.

The topic of Sheriff Buff Lamb somehow came up. While the two men waited in their van, Greene County Deputy James Shaw allegedly heard one man say that Sheriff Lamb was *"crazy in the head and that he was going to shoot him by morning!"*

Shaw further stated that the van sped around another car but was stopped a few minutes later. Shaw called Christian County Sheriff, Buff Lamb, on the radio and told him what the man had said. Buff told Shaw to hold the man until he arrived.

When Sheriff Lamb arrived, it is this writer's opinion that every lawman within a country mile had a smile on his face. They knew what was coming. Everyone had heard of Sheriff L. E. (Buff) Lamb of Christian County. He was a living legend in Missouri, with a reputation taller than a New York skyscraper.

Threatening Buff Lamb was like throwing a rock at a grizzly bear; why would you want to do that? Buff and his deputies stated he asked the man to step out of the car and walk with him. Lamb further stated that the man turned to strike him, so he struck first with his baton.

Deputy Gale Clinton reported it this way: "We heard radio traffic to stop a white Volkswagen. A van with no license plate, but a Tennessee permit in the rear window. And that the driver had threatened to kill Buff Lamb before the night was over. We turned around. Upon arriving, we saw the vehicle, and Greene County Deputies had the two subjects out of the vehicle. They were standing on the right passenger side of the vehicle."

"I spoke to the subject and asked him why he wanted to kill Buff Lamb. He didn't give me an answer. I then asked the passenger what his name was, and he said, "[101]Clyde Johnson". I asked him if he had been drinking, and his answer was "I'm twenty-four years old and I can [102]drink if I want to!" Buff showed up twenty to thirty minutes later.

"Who's the man that wants to kill me?" bellowed Buff.

Gale Clinton pointed at the man.

"Do you know me?"

"No."

---

[101] Name withheld.

[102] Mr. Clinton would say in court that the individual "was so unsteady, he could hardly stand without rocking, nor hold his eyes open".

"Then why do you want to kill me?"

"I don't like the way you treat kids who come down to Christian County to party."

"That's none of your damn business! You'd better get in your car and go home if you don't want your head skinned!" Buff turned, took two steps, and stopped.

"I ain't scared! Nobody's going to skin my head!"

Buff turned around and walked back to Terrel. "Let's go out to the bank here and talk about it." The man walked away with the sheriff but stumbled and fell in a ditch. He got up and walked about fifteen more feet with Buff and stopped. The two argued.

"Then I saw [103]Terrel grab Buff's left arm and closed my eyes and shuddered. When I opened my eyes, Terrel was on the ground, at his feet, laying by a telephone pole. He laid there a short time, and I walked over to check Terrel to see if he was alright. I rolled Terrel over, and he started getting up."

"You have no business threatening the life of an officer!" said Buff.

"I'm mad because Greene County called some Negroes, Niggers!"

"I ain't got nothing to do with that! I don't ever want to see you up here again. If I do, you'd better kill me!"

The man's story differed from Buff's. He stated Buff struck him without provocation. He also stated that he went to a hospital because of his injury. These are his words from an interview: "...I got stopped on a Friday night, it was my birthday, and uh, there was a wreck with a wrecker pulled across the highway, and you had no option but to wait on them. Then this deputy walked up to my window and said, 'It's just a bunch of niggers. We'll have them out of your way in a minute.' When I left there, he radioed in that I had threatened to kill Buff Lamb before morning, and tried to run over him. . .and what I did tell the guy? Yeah. I'm in a National Guard Unit in Springfield, and a lot of the guys are from Ozark, and they're always talking how Buff beats up people, and one of these days someone will get him for it."

Bill and I had been drinking all afternoon but they never did search our car...Crack... and when I woke up, he was kicking me

---

[103] Name withheld.

and I was bleeding all over the place…he was standing there with his broken nightstick, there was blood on it. He was waving it around like he was at some KKK meeting…you get your ass in your car and get out of here…"

As the Rock Festival wound down according to one reporter, Buff had a German Shepard dog with him. The dog allegedly snarled at people's heels while Buff told them to hurry and move on.

When Sheriff Owens learned what Buff was doing, he allegedly stated, "Buff gets carried away sometimes."

One reporter alleged Owen's deputies brandished baseball bats. And that Sheriff Owens made jokes about it. Did it really happen? Only those at the festival know for sure.

One year later, the man sued Sheriff Owen and Sheriff Lamb. The suit ended in a mistrial with eleven jurors for Terrel, and one against.

"The Judge didn't believe Buff was acting in self-defense. Not with twenty-three squad cars and deputies standing around." said by a victim in a 2019 interview.

The next month, Terrel sued again. The Sheriff's bonding companies settled with Terrel for an undisclosed amount. The man stated that he received a few thousand dollars ($3,000?) from Buff.

Boasting in a taped interview, Terrel claimed the judge made Sheriff Owens cry for the last 3 days in court. "The Federal Judge told him (Sheriff Owen) if you lie to me one more time, I'm going to lock you up for a long time."

It's hard to imagine Sheriff Mickey Owen sobbing in court, but that's what Terrel says happened.

Terrel claimed that the wallop he took from Sheriff Lamb gave him nightmares. For years! Anyone from law enforcement, corrections, care facilities, emergency personnel, or any soldier, would have trouble understanding how one incident could affect an individual so severely. But Terrel was no ordinary individual, and a renowned sheriff striking him was more than his constitution could digest.

Another man on the same panel stated he had spent two weeks in Buff's jail, and that Buff was nice to him the entire time. "He wasn't out of character at all, but I didn't threaten to kill him or anything. The last time I saw Buff, he was one of the nicest guys you'd ever want to be around."

As for Buff, after blacking out at his home, Buff's wife admitted him to a hospital in Springfield. He stayed there for four days. The stress of his job and Terrel's lawsuits could have caused the blackouts. No one knows for sure.

In 2015, while on a panel with former Festival Organizers, Terrel stated he had become infamous as the man who 'got his head bashed in the day of the concert'.

With his notoriety, he and his family attended the Route 66 Concerts for five years. "They basically gave us anything we wanted," said Terrel boastingly.

While no doubt assaulted by the sheriff, the assault made the [104]victim a footnote in history. Otherwise, Terrel may have drifted into anonymity like the rest of us.

After the lawsuit, you'd have thought Sheriff Lamb would have slowed down—but not Buff Lamb. He was determined to keep Christian County as safe and drug-free as possible.

After noise complaints at Lindenlure, a popular party spot for kids, Sheriff Lamb arrived and told a boy to turn down the music. When the boy hesitated and took his time, the Sheriff shot a hole through the boy's stereo box.

When Buff Lamb gave you an order, he meant for you to follow it! Not later--now!

Former Lamb Deputy, Wandal Heatherly. recalled an incident at Lindenlure.

"One big boy, 250-260 pounds, sitting on the hood of a car, mouthed off to Buff and said, *"F...you!"* Buff told the boy he had three minutes to get out of there! Buff swatted the boy on the butt with a blackjack as he got in the car."

The next morning, Sunday, the boy's Momma showed up

---

[104] Sheriff Lamb struck the man and damaged him physically and mentally. The victim states he had nightmares for years. The soldiers returning from Vietnam during this time, had been tortured and endured mental and physical suffering beyond comprehension. They came home from the jungles of Southeast Asia and would have some HELLISH nightmares to work through. Buff was financially hurt by the incident. In fact, some would say it cost him an election as well.

because he had told her that Buff had beaten him. Nothing could have been further from the truth. But in those days, it was an honor of sorts to brag that you had taken a beating from the infamous Sheriff Buff Lamb.

"It didn't happen that way, Ma'am. Yeah, I swatted him. He told me to go F Myself. I kicked his butt and told him to get out of there!" The woman stared into the sheriff's eyes for a moment and then turned and skirted out of the office.

Buff searching vehicle

Chapter Fifteen

A KINDER, GENTLER LAWMAN

January 1972, Deputies Harold Wampler, and Wallace Groover, searched the home of Frank Rinker. What they found turned out to be the largest stash of stolen goods in Christian County's history.

There were so many items that it was impossible to load and bring them into the sheriff's office. To view the items, they took victims to the house to identify their property. They had items stolen from Texas, Stone, Greene, Lawrence, St. Clair, and Christian counties. Buff's deputies were always on the job.

Friday, February 11, 1972, Buff boarded a plane along with Highway Patrolman Wayne Murphy. They were on their way to Davenport, Iowa.

Sheriff Lamb had received some vital information. A prisoner had been shooting his mouth off about the 1969 Carol Blades murder. The man allegedly knew who the killer was.

Having lived in Mountain Grove, Missouri, the prisoner knew the area. In 1954, he had been arrested him in Christian County for burglary.

After interviewing the man, Buff was sure he was not the murderer. The prisoner lacked details of the crime, and his story was inconsistent. The Law Enforcement officers believed his information had come from news clippings. Or could it have been from another prisoner? Either way, his information was discounted.

Back in Ozark, Chief [105]Ray Speak observed a suspicious vehicle behind the Western Auto store. When he neared the car, it sped away at a high rate of speed, and Ray gave chase.

The car reached speeds of over 100 mph. The chase ended when Ray crashed his car into the suspect's sedan. The car was totaled, and the two suspects ran into the brush.

[106]Ray was cut and bruised. It took a moment for him to collect his senses and call for help. While Ray waited for backup, he stumbled around in the dark, checking the suspect's abandoned car. He was bleeding and unstable on his feet. He was on the verge of blacking out. Hopefully, help would arrive soon before the lights went out.

Near the suspect's car, Ray found a man's wallet. When help arrived, the lawmen discovered the boys had stolen the car from Joe Kenyion of Sparta. Ray Speak was treated at Cox Hospital in Springfield, for minor injuries.

Ray was a tough and daring lawman. When he wasn't keeping the law in Ozark, he was a competitive motorcycle and stock car driver.

Twenty-one days after Ray's accident, several candidates entered the race for sheriff. They were: Joe Mayberry, Luther Meadows, Pletcher Rogers, [107]Raymond Gold, former Sheriff Jack Monger, and Buff Lamb. Only two had a chance of beating the Sheriff; Jack Monger and Joe Mayberry.

By August, the Republican Primary [108]elected Joe Mayberry. The county had spoken.

Several incidents had hurt Buff's election. There was his implication in the unsolved murder of Carol Blades. The lawsuit for striking someone with a baton. And the rumors of brutality and heavy-handed justice. These all weighed heavily on the minds of

---

[105] Throughout interviews with numerous people, this writer was told that you can believe 100% of what Ray Speak says. People considered him honest and knowledgeable about Buff Lamb.

[106] Chief of Police Ray Speak was as tough as they come. I worked with Ray's son-in-law, Mark and he is a great guy as well.

[107] Missouri Senator Tom Eagleton recommended Gold for the job of Sheriff.

[108] Mayberry beat Buff Lamb by just 52 votes in the Republican Primary.

voters.

It was time for a change. For Christian County to grow, it needed a kinder and gentler approach to law enforcement. Joe Mayberry was the man to usher in that growth.

Mayberry disapproved of Buff's fear tactics and alleged [109]flashlight justice. He believed people should like you, not fear you.

Buff believed criminals equated kindness to weakness. Toughness with strength, and vulnerability to easy pickings. But no matter what he thought, Mayberry was in and Buff was out. It was time for Buff to find another job or face the unemployment line.

After a Middle East embargo on oil, President Nixon agreed to open a pipeline to the U.S. from Alaska. Work on the pipeline began in 1974.

"Clara, I can make a lot of money out there. Besides, I'll get to do some hunting! Maybe kill a bear or moose!"

"I dunno, Buff..."

"It'll be fine. Besides Jack (Monger) and Knial Iorg might go with me!"

Just like that, Buff Lamb was in Alaska at the end of 1974, working as a powder monkey and drill man.

His job comprised of drilling holes in the ground and setting off dynamite charges. It was one of the most dangerous jobs on the pipeline, but it paid well.

It took powerful arms and nerves of steel to blow up mountains and enormous holes in the ground. Both of which Buff had honed as a daredevil and lawman.

By now, Buff was fifty and Jack Monger was forty-nine. The men sometimes slept in tent cities, braving cold days and nights. The air was clean and crisp, and the countryside was breathtakingly beautiful.

With twenty hours of daylight, sleep came through exhausting days of work with brief rest. Because of the remote country, the supplies came by pack mules. The two men were living among the

---

[109] Buff Lamb allegedly carried and beat lawbreakers with a five-cell flashlight he carried. Wyatt Earp allegedly used the butt of a pistol and Buford Pusser a big stick. Buff would forever be characterized as a lawman who wielded a flashlight.

bears, wolves, and mountain lions. Buff was living the life of a 19th-century frontiersman.

Back in Christian County, they received eight to fourteen inches of rain in July. The area flooded. The waters kept Sheriff Mayberry and Police Chief Ray Speak busy checking on people.

On a Saturday in October 1974, the dispatcher called Sheriff Mayberry.

"Dispatch to Sheriff Mayberry."

"Go ahead dispatch."

"The trailer park manager called and said a tenant killed a man and his estranged wife. The shooter is in his trailer."

"Ten-four, I'm on my way."

When the sheriff arrived, he knocked on the trailer house door and heard a weak *'come in'*. Inside sat Clifton Hartsgrove, who admitted to killing his wife and her lover.

Hartsgrove had followed his wife and her boyfriend to Christian County from Ohio. He shot the couple with a .38 caliber pistol. They found his wife in the bathroom, her lover in the bedroom. Hartsgrove's five children saw the shooting.

[110]Clifton gave up without a fight. They arrested him and locked him in the Ozark jail. Eight months later, Clifton, along with three other men, escaped by picking the lock on their cell door.

The killer had changed his mind about spending the rest of his life in prison. He was a fugitive on the run from Ozark, but not for long.

Hartsgrove was captured and sent to the Missouri State Penitentiary. He received 12 years for each of the two murders.

By the end of his second year in office, popularity issues beset Sheriff Mayberry. Like Buff, he had his way of running the Sheriff's office. And cooperating with fellow law enforcement agencies wasn't in his plans. There was also talk of an investigation by the Attorney General's Office regarding Sheriff Mayberry's job performance. But that never happened.

Ozark Police Officer, Pletcher Rogers was suing the Sheriff Mayberry in Federal Court claiming harassment by the sheriff and

---

[110] Nixa Police Chief Jack Savage stated that he offered to assist the Sheriff, but Mayberry turned him down. Savage believed he may have been able to stop the killing if the sheriff would have accepted his offer.

his deputy. Rogers also claimed that the sheriff was interfering with their police duties.

[111]Other claims: Mayberry declined help from local law enforcement officers. He had fired five deputies whom he thought still supported the former sheriff Buff Lamb. He refused to hand out deputy commissions to area lawmen. And, according to Ozark's Mayor, he would not allow the city police to lock prisoners in his jail.

In response, Mayberry stated, "There's no need to commission them. The former sheriff (Buff Lamb) commissioned the Ozark Police for political power."

Rogers' lawsuit against [112]Mayberry was dismissed by an out-of-court settlement in 1977.

During his reign as sheriff, Mayberry worked several shootings and nuisance crimes. As the next election drew closer, a rumor spread; Crime in Christian County was the worst it had ever been.

Dead bodies were turning up, and many believed Mayberry was partly to blame. Locals believed Mayberry's softer approach to crime had weakened the county.

"I remember Mayberry would look out the courthouse window and holler. "Now you boys better stop that!" He wouldn't even get out of his chair to see what was going on!" --Resident of Ozark.

"Mayberry had a car stopped one time, the man hollered at him and Mayberry got back in his car and left!" --Another resident of Ozark

"With Buff gone, crime moved in!"— (name withheld).

"All we had was lawlessness with Mayberry."— (name withheld).

To his credit, Mayberry helped eradicate marijuana and drugs in the county. He also worked some hard cases, discovering a man shot in the back of his head, and another electrocuted in the power lines.

Sheriff Mayberry did his best to serve the law. The problem was when "he" was sheriff, Buff had thrown a huge rope over Christian

---

[111] It was reported that some law enforcement officers and citizens wanted Sheriff Mayberry to face a Grand Jury and be impeached. Some wanted him investigated by the Attorney General's Office.

[112] Mayberry's deputy had served papers on Rogers for passing bad checks. But he denied arresting him.

County.

Would-be criminals did their haranguing elsewhere while Buff was in office. Buff's reputation as a tough lawman was enough to keep criminals out of Christian County. But Buff wasn't the sheriff anymore, Joe Mayberry was.

Unfortunately for Sheriff Mayberry in 1976, crime soared in Christian County. There were break-ins, vandalism, drugs, and stealing. There was no sugarcoating it. Crime was running rampant in Christian County, and a few people believed it was because Buff was gone.

Some believed Mayberry opened the door, and the criminals walked through it. To the sheriff's supporters, the crime wave was no one's fault except the criminals who perpetrated them. Unfortunately, the Sheriff and his men felt the brunt of people's dissatisfaction. It didn't matter that the department had made twenty-three arrests.

It was in March 1976, when Joe Mayberry's deputy found a body shot in the back of the head. He discovered the body along Highway 65, about three miles outside of town.

Later that day, they arrested two suspects in the murder. Rumors spread that dead bodies were showing up all over Christian County.

One former Springfield Police Officer (L.B.) said that it was a standing joke around the Springfield P.D. "If you found a dead body and needed rid of it, you took it to Christian County. They were used to dealing with murders."

But L.B. wasn't the only one who saw the rise in murders. Surrounding counties gossiped about how rough and criminally populated Ozark had become. Something had to give. Christian County was earning a dangerous reputation. A reputation as a haven for crime and a crow's nest for Missouri criminals.

In Alaska, Buff suffered a major injury to his legs when a stack of dynamite cases fell on him. His legs were already crippled from car wrecks and bull riding. Now he was back in the hospital with another injury.

Buff was finding it harder and harder to walk. The pain he lived with day to day was tormenting. A lesser man would have quit, but not Buff Lamb.

Later that year, sheriff Mayberry was in the news for raiding another marijuana field. You never knew what Joe Mayberry would do. Sometimes he appeared soft on crime, other times he was no nonsense. Take for instance this next story.

While raiding an alleged pot field, George White of Nixa refused to come out of his house. Sheriff Mayberry showed caliber when he gave the order to lob gas grenades into the man's home. White quickly surrendered.

Buff Lamb returned from the pipeline and set about campaigning for sheriff. He attended chili suppers, spoke at meetings, and went door to door to ask for people's votes.

"You've seen what it's been like under Mayberry's administration. Crime in this county has soared. Make me your sheriff again and I will send the thugs and dope peddlers packing! You have my word!"

Buff won the 1976 Republican Primary by a [113]landslide. The voters wanted a man who would be tougher on crime and NO ONE, I mean NO ONE, was tougher than Louard Elbert "Buff" Lamb.

[114]Sheriff Joe Mayberry left the office, never to run again. He had done his best for Christian County. If not for him, Christian County would have dropped into a huge sinkhole of marijuana growers. But a lot of people were glad when he was gone. Former Nixa Police Chief, Jack Savage, said he was treated better by the prisoners he took to jail than he was by Sheriff Joe Mayberry.

January 1977, Sheriff Lamb was sworn into office. He never wanted to leave in the first place. And this time, he was coming back with the sword of vengeance. There was just one problem. A man was threatening to kill Buff if he was re-elected.

---

[113] In the Republican Primary, Buff beat Mayberry by 1,236 votes.
[114] Former Christian County Sheriff Joe Mayberry passed away in January 1977. He was 75 years old. He had been a farmer, Real Estate Agent, and Presiding Judge in Lawrence County. His presence in this world will always be missed.

CHAPTER SIXTEEN

LINDENLURE

"And I want the partying and drugs down at Lindenlure to stop! I am going to rid this county of drugs, killings, car thieves, and cattle rustlers, and I aim to do it starting now! I want the word to go out–Mayberry is gone. Buff Lamb is back! If you break the law in my county, we are coming after you. Any questions?"

"No Sir!"

"Good. We're stepping up the raids at Lindenlure and if you hear there are drugs in my county, I want to know about it!"

"Yes Sir!"

"Now get out there and get to work!"

The men left feeling like an all-state football team in a locker room at halftime. They had their marching orders. Get out there and take Christian County back from the thugs and criminals.

That evening, the newly re-elected sheriff started for the door to go on night patrol.

"Wait a minute, Buff, where are you going?" asked Wandal Heatherly.

"On patrol, why?"

"Have you forgotten what the Highway Patrol said? There's a man out there who says he's going to kill you tonight!"

"Oh yeah, I forgot," Buff walked over to a gun cabinet and retrieved a sawed-off shotgun.

"I'm going with you if you don't mind?"

"Now Wandal I'll be..."

"You know I'm a crack shot. I'm going with you!"

"Sure, let's go."

Buff knew there was no point arguing. His men cared about him, and any of them would have taken a bullet for him.

"The hitman was from Kansas City. The guy had set the date and time when he was going to kill Buff. They were going to kill him in the Sheriff's zone (parking) on the south side of the square."

"Once in the patrol car, he put it (sawed-off shotgun) underneath his seat. Buff was going to go alone, so I went with him."

"By about 11 pm, Buff was sound asleep. Buff put in so many hours a day, he could never stay awake. I gave people the "eyeball" when they drove by, but nothing happened. A few days later, the FBI heard about Buff's illegal shotgun and came and confiscated it." --Wandal Heatherly, 2015

Down at Lindenlure, a favorite river party spot, Buff arrived one night and ordered a boy to turn down his loud music. When the boy refused, Buff shot the music box, blowing it to bits with a shotgun.

The blast got the party-goers' attention, and they packed their stuff in a hurry. Buff and his deputies were not messing around! Most stories circulated about Buff in the 1970s were based on incidents like this one.

Buff came down hard on the [115]kids for drinking and drugging, and the stories about him grew and grew. Lindenlure had become the chosen party spot for kids all over the country.

Friday thru Sunday there was always a campfire and party along the river. Kids socialized, drank, forged romances, and sometimes smoked and inhaled drugs.

When Buff became sheriff for the second time, he declared a war on drugs. Lindenlure became a focal point, and he and his deputies gave it a lot of attention.

---

[115] Most people in the area believed that Buff hated kids. This writer does not believe that. Buff hated to see kids ruin their lives with drugs and alcohol. He was sometimes tough on kids, but it was because he cared about them.

Some locals thought Buff hated kids because of the way he treated them down at Lindenlure. The truth is, he loved kids and he was doing his best to protect them. And he did it with a stern hand.

Sheriff Lamb wasn't the only one tough on crime. Buff expected his deputies to be hard as nails, too. Buff wanted people to respect the law and live within its boundaries. If they did, they'd have no trouble with the sheriff's department.

Charlie Hammer remembered the time he met Buff as a teenager: "One evening while cruising the square with two of my friends, we saw Buff and one of his deputies. One boy in the car stuck out his hand to make a sign that two cops were watching the town square. A *big* mistake for him! The Deputy and Buff pulled us over. Buff stood back while the deputy read us the riot act! After that, we left Ozark and never returned!"

Few people knew it, even his deputies, but Buff drank. He didn't carry a bottle around with him, but on occasion, he'd slip off and have a drink or two. But he was very discrete about it. This was remembered by one Ozark city employee:

"I remember when my parents operated a package store (liquor) and Buff was a frequent customer. Buff never went inside the store; he always drove around back and received his drink in a paper bag."

As for womanizing, it's not clear when, and if, Buff ever stopped chasing women. A dispatcher from another county remembered when Buff took her and a co-worker to dinner.

"Buff had been drinking when he asked me to dance, and I politely refused."

"No woman turns me down!" bellowed the imbibed sheriff.

"Well, I am!"

"The next day Buff walked into the office and wanted to see the Sheriff! I told him he was in his office. I thought for sure I was in trouble for turning Buff down. I didn't know what he was going to tell the sheriff!"

"A few minutes later Buff exited the sheriff's office, looked down at me, and turned toward the sheriff."

"Oh, by the way, I have a lot of respect for [116]Donna she turned

---

[116] Not her real name. But this writer knew Donna when she was a dispatcher and was friends with her daughter.

me down for a dance, but I have a lot of respect for her!"

"Yes, we like her around here," the sheriff said. —Deputy's name withheld.

Another time while still married to Clara, Buff asked a local law enforcement officer to set him up with a woman they both knew. It is doubtful Buff ever stopped cheating on any of his wives to this point.

Regarding toughness, Buff Lamb not only talked the talk, but he walked the walk. Buff was all sand and bravado. Take for instance this next story by a former deputy.

"Buff got a domestic call about an armed man who was threatening his wife. When Buff and I arrived, we saw the man had taped a revolver in each hand."

"Instead of drawing his weapon and taking cover behind his car, Buff walked up to the man. The man cocked the hammers of his pistols and pointed them at Buff. Buff would have been within his rights to shoot and kill the man in self-defense, but he didn't!"

"Don't take another step, Sheriff or I'll...I'll...I'll blow your head off!" said the man.

"You don't want to shoot me. [117]Bill and I don't want to die. I just want to talk to you."

"Buff continued to talk to the man, and from time to time he would cock and then un-cock his pistols. He could have killed Buff anytime he wanted. And Buff could have shot him, and nobody would have said a thing. There were some tense moments, but Buff talked him into giving up. Buff had a lot of guts!"

"In those days, we worked cases where we'd get a call about a drunk with a shotgun. But we didn't call for backup, and we didn't shoot anyone. We even went to other counties to make arrests when the sheriff of that county was afraid to! Those counties knew that if they called Buff, he'd come, or send one of us." --Wandal Heatherly, 2015

Wandal recalled the time he and Buff went to [118]Wayward County to arrest a man on a warrant. The county sheriff refused to serve the warrant. He said the man was "too dangerous".

---

[117] Real name withheld.
[118] Not the real county.

"That nut is armed, mentally unstable, and I need him picked up for an evaluation. He's going to shoot someone if they go out there. He's got a lot of guns."

"My men and I can pick him up!" said Buff.

"I'd sure appreciate it. If I show up, he'll kill me! He lives down there on...."

"When we got there, it was dark, and we crept up on the porch and looked inside. We saw a man sleeping on the couch, and there were guns everywhere! Buff banged on the front door and we watched the man get off the couch and come to the door. Our biggest concern was that he'd go for a gun. Buff looked back at us, "You boys wait out here. I'll call you if I need you."

"Buff went in and sat in a chair while the man sat on the couch. Ten minutes passed when we slapped our hands against our revolvers. The man reached for something under the couch cushion, and Buff wasn't moving. We thought for sure he was reaching for a pistol!"

"As it turned out, the man was retrieving a pint of whiskey. Buff had told him he could have a drink before we left. The sheriff brought the man outside, who seemed worried about someone taking his car. Buff walked over to the car, opened the hood, lifted the distributor cap, and pulled off the rotor. He stuck it in his pants pocket. Buff told the man, "I'll make sure they don't take it!"

"Buff knew how to talk to people, and regardless of what people said, he was not a bad guy."

Like most people, Buff Lamb had his share of faults. But if someone was breaking into your house, it was Buff Lamb you wanted to show up on your front porch. Not some forgiving, by-the-book, liberal sheriff.

With their chests stuck out and their backs straight as a board, people called Buff Lamb "their friend" and said it with pride. It was like being the friend of Wyatt Earp or Bat Masterson of the old west. Buff was a celebrity in southwest Missouri. The people who liked Buff's toughness would tell you he was the best Sheriff Christian County ever had!

Being Buff Lamb's friend was something to boast about. People in small communities in the 50's, the 60's, and 70's wanted justice. How it was gotten didn't matter, providing it was served. And no one was better at battling crime than Sheriff Buff Lamb.

CHAPTER SEVENTEEN

IT'S TIME FOR THE SHERIFF TO GO!

The bodies sat in the plane, like mannequins in a department store window. The scene? Surreal and haunting. Inside the plane wreckage sat six bodies still buckled in their seats.

As Sheriff Buff Lamb, Jack Savage, and [119]Larry Baker arrived at the site near Boaz in Christian County, they were shaken by what they saw.

If not for the blood, the disheveled travelers looked like they were asleep. Baker recalled that one cadaver had an airplane shaft driven through his chest. It exited out of his back.

It was a scene that could creep into your subconsciousness and stay hidden for a while. But come alive in your nightmares when you least expected it.

The odor of fuel and burnt wiring filled the lawman's nostrils while he helped extract bodies from the plane. Baker had this to say about that day: "I couldn't get the smell of those dead bodies out of my clothes." A lawman's job was full of unpleasant tasks, and that was one of them.

In the middle 1970's, two troublemakers from Springfield met (probably over drinks) and decided that Sheriff Buff Lamb of

---

[119] The real person ask that I not give their name.

Christian County needed to be stopped... "permanently."

After much deliberation on how and when they would kill the sheriff, the two decided to kill Buff on his birthday. Not only that, but they'd kill him on the courthouse lawn for all to see. That, my friend, takes a lot of hate.

As the day of the ambush grew closer and closer, one assassin told a friend about their plans, who in turn, told a Christian County Deputy.

The deputy alerted Buff, who promptly alerted a Springfield Detective. The former jailbirds were brought in for questioning, and the murder attempt was thwarted.

The two hitmen were never seen or heard from again. And warned that if they ever stepped foot in Christian County again, they'd never leave there alive.

On a chilly day in September 1978, Buff was en route to a fatal highway accident when a car came racing toward him. Instinctively, Buff jerked the steering wheel at the last possible second.

He missed the driver but skidded off the road, through a fence, and overturned his car in a farmer's field. The driver of the other vehicle sped away at a high rate of speed.

Buff's car sat in the field, eerily and upside down, the front wheels still spinning. Luckily, he had been thrown from the wreckage where he lay with broken ribs and numerous cuts and bruises. He was unable to move, and his breathing was labored. He was hurt badly, but he'd live.

Nancy Young, an ambulance driver, recalled carrying Buff out of the field into the ambulance. "Boy, was he heavy!" She later recalled. "Buff had been in several wrecks. This was not the first or last time I helped lift the sheriff into the ambulance. He was well known for wrecking patrol cars."

The number of wrecks Buff survived as a lawman is perplexing. How could a former stunt driver, accustomed to driving cars, working on cars, and pushing cars to their limits, have so many near-fatal accidents?

One former friend who rode with Buff stated, "It was different back then. You know how it was. Most of the roads were gravel, and it was easy to slide off the road in a high-speed chase!"

And yet, Buff presumably knew how to handle a car better than anyone in the state. Is it possible that someone was deliberately running Buff off the road? Buff had his share of enemies, and some of those wanted the sheriff *dead*.

It would come as no surprise to Christian County if they awakened one morning to hear that Buff had been killed or murdered. Buff was prolific, aggressive, and a menace to the wrong people. Buff stood up when others sat down. He charged ahead when others stood still. Killing Buff Lamb would be a notch on any gunman's pistol.

A few days later, his broken ribs taped, the 54-year-old Sheriff was back on the job. He and his men were in the fields hunting and destroying marijuana plants.

As fast as the calls came in, Buff was in the brush with the ticks, chiggers, and venomous snakes hunting down the devil weed patches. "I just hated that dope!" Buff said, referencing marijuana.

Partying on Swan Creek one night near Busiek Park ,[120]G.A. and his cousin had never heard of Sheriff Buff Lamb until he walked up to their vehicle. Buff ordered G. A. to open an 8-track cassette box when his cousin popped off, "Don't do it! It's full of marijuana and cocaine!"

Buff walked around to the boy and grabbed him by the collar. His flashlight was in his right hand. Buff bellowed, "I'll give you flashlight surgery and feed you to the crawdads! Now git out of here!" The boys quickly left!

When 1980 rolled around, Buff announced that he would run for sheriff again, but if elected, he would retire at the end of his term.

The news came as a shock to Christian County citizens. By this time, Buff Lamb was a southern Missouri icon. His retirement would mean the end of an era of tough law enforcement.

Bill Ramsey and Joe Tatum announced their bid for sheriff. [121]Bill Ramsey, the Ozark Chief of Police, claimed he had been urged to run by all of his friends.

Tatum's posters read: *"Harassment and arrest without*

---

[120] Name withheld. The individual later became a Springfield, Police Officer.
[121] Roughly a year later, Mayor Howard Jones ousted Bill Ramsey as Chief of Police, and gave the job to Pletcher Rogers whom he had hand-picked for the job.

evidence, cost tax dollars." Locals thought the posters were aimed at Sheriff Lamb, and they were.

On a frosty night in January, Buff responded to a house fire in Ozark. Volunteer firemen and Buff did all they could to save the family in the house. But the fire killed a woman, her husband, and their thirteen-year-old boy.

The sight and smell of the burnt bodies were more than Buff could handle. The ghastly images of the family amongst the smoldering debris, haunted Buff in his dreams.

He found it hard to sleep and drank more than he ever had. "It was terrible to see that boy's body," Buff said.

On May 28th someone dynamited Ozark's telephone tower. It was estimated that 50-60 pounds of explosives were used. Who would do such a thing? Was someone mad at the phone company? Like a good sheriff, Buff was there to investigate the sabotage. The damages exceeded $500,000.

The following month, Buff was in the hospital for gallbladder surgery. Problems with his gall bladder had caused the doctors to work on him twice that year.

At 56, Buff was slowing down, aging fast, and relying more on his deputies. He was not as strong as he once was. His legs were crippled, but he was still the big buck of the woods. His name alone carried the weight of a thousand-pound bull. His reputation as a seasoned lawman proceeded him like an impending storm on the horizon.

In June, after numerous complaints about the noise and drugs down at Lindenlure, Buff had to do something.

"I'm not going to keep putting up with those people. I get tired of going there on Sunday afternoon to babysit a bunch of potheads! We're going to move in and stop every bit of it if we have to arrest a hundred of them!" Sheriff Lamb said.

In July 1980, a newcomer threw his hat into the ring for sheriff, Billy L. Wright. Wright had served two tours in Europe during World War II and had lots of friends in Ozark.

But as popular as he was, Christian County believed there was only one man for the job — "Buff Lamb!" August 2nd of 1980 rolled around and the former marshal and sheriff won the Republican Primary.

It was his third time winning an election. Sheriff Lamb

continued his war on drugs. After 12 days in office, he and his men raided another marijuana field worth $528,000. Over half a million dollars!

The growers were not captured, but the weed was taken off the streets and out of the hands of young users.

A few days later, Sheriff Lamb raided a two-story building where marijuana was being grown. Christian County had become one of the largest pot producers in the Midwest. Sheriff Lamb and his deputies were working day and night to eradicate the drug problem.

That same month, November, Sheriff Lamb stepped outside of his home about 10:30 pm and found his truck had been stolen. Someone had come to the sheriff's house and stolen his truck while he sat in his recliner. That was a death wish. Who in the world would be so stupid. . .or brave?

Buff called the Highway Patrol and by 10:45 he received a call back from his dispatcher. "Sheriff, they've found your Suburban."

"Where's it at and who the took it?"

"Sheriff. . .the Highway Patrol says it's down by the old gravel pit under the bridge, north of the Taney County line. Sheriff, the truck is burned to a crisp."

"That *son-of-a-bitch*!" A few minutes later, Buff hung up the phone.

"What's wrong, Buff?"

"Go back to bed, Clara. My truck has been stolen and burned. Orvil is on his way over to pick me up. I'll take care of this. Get some rest. I'll call you later."

It was not the first time the sheriff's truck had been stolen.

"We had a trustee in the jail who I didn't trust. When I overheard him talking about making an escape, I told Buff about it the next morning."

"Oh, I don't think he'll do that Danny (Clinton). He seems to be okay around here."

"Not long after that, a reserve dispatcher, whom I had loaned a pistol to because he didn't have one, was working when the trustee made his move. The dispatcher had left the pistol in a drawer instead of wearing it and went to the restroom. When he returned, the trustee had the gun.

"I'm taking your gun, this jacket (Buff's), and that car down there (Buff's). I don't want to hurt you, Virgil, but I will if I have to."

The trustee escaped but was captured in Springfield, with Danny Clinton's gun. Luckily, Buff got his car back—that time.

Was burning the sheriff's truck a high school prank? A few people thought so and dismissed it as adolescent shenanigans. Or was someone trying to send a message to the arrogant sheriff? Whoever did it, didn't leave any clues. Maybe they wanted Buff to know that he was not indestructible, and they could get to him if they wanted.

The facts were, that someone had threatened to kill Buff if he was re-elected. Soon after that, Buff was run off the road by an unknown person(s) and now his truck had been stolen and charred. They say bad news comes in three's—ordinarily, but there was nothing ordinary about Buff Lamb.

Like the Postal Service, neither snow, nor rain, nor heat, nor gloom of night could keep Buff from his rounds, and performance of his duties. The lawman spent eighteen hours a day working and rarely slept.

In December, Buff arrested a United States fugitive living in Ozark under an assumed name. He had been in Ozark for eleven years!

Early in 1981, [122]Glenn Spencer, a pastor in Taney County approached Buff. "Sheriff, I need a deputy's commission. I carry large sums of money because of my business, and I'm worried I might get robbed."

"What kind of business do you have Glenn?"

"I sell farm equipment. I have an implement business."

"Come by this afternoon and I'll swear you in."

"Thanks, Sheriff, I'll see you this afternoon!"

When Joe Mayberry was in office, they said you couldn't squeeze a commission out of him. But Buff Lamb wasn't Joe Mayberry. It made Buff feel important to hand out commissions.

"Back then, Buff handed out deputy commissions like they were candy. All you had to do was ask, and tell him why you needed a gun permit, and he'd hand you a commission!" This was said by a former law enforcement officer from Ozark.

---

[122] Name withheld.

As hard as Buff tried to help people, a few people despised, scorned, and mocked him. It's been said that you can't make an omelet without cracking a few eggs. Sheriff Lamb had cracked his share of egos and bad tempers.

By this time in his career, nefarious miscreants cursed and reviled the sheriff. A few even wanted him *dead*. Buff had cost criminals millions of dollars in stolen merchandise and drugs. It was worse than the old moonshine wars, this was a war on drugs and Buff was winning.

In keeping the County safe, Buff had made himself a target for all the bad guys in the Midwest. As for Glenn Spencer, the former businessman, and preacher, Buff pulled his gun permit when he heard Spencer was involved in some illegal activity.

A week later, Buff arrested Spencer for re-selling farm equipment he knew had been stolen. Spencer allegedly had a [123] gang of five people who stole tractors for him. He re-sold the tractors at his implement store.

They estimated Spencer had received at least 70 stolen tractors. With self-righteous indignation, Spencer spewed out hatred for Buff Lamb and the sheriff's department. He criticized Buff to anyone who would listen.

Spencer made it clear that he would not roll over and take his arrest laying down! He was determined to see the arrogant sheriff brought down to his knees!

Glenn Spencer would, as it turned out, have to wait in line. There were pot growers, thieves, and purported tough guys who wanted a piece of the sheriff first.

The Sheriff and his deputies were hauling marijuana crops in by truckloads. As quickly as they planted a pot field, Buff's informers helped him solve cases. If that failed, he kept watch on suspects and brought them in for questioning. If that failed, he resorted to more drastic means of extricating [124] information.

---

[123] If he had a gang, that's 5 people's pockets Buff was getting into. Five people who might want the sheriff out of the way.

[124] Three separate individuals stated they were present when Buff used old-fashioned southern techniques for extracting information. It was a common means to

To successfully get information that could solve many crimes or save lives, Buff used a technique that had been around for a thousand years; he used torture. Rarely and only on rare occasions, but he did what he felt he had to do to get the truth from unwilling participants.

According to a witness, Buff forced a man to sit in a chair and stretch out his legs onto another chair, forming a bridge. Buff would sit on the man's legs causing excruciating pain to him. It was a scene from a 1950's Alabama jail. But in this case, Buff was the fat, badge-toting country sheriff with the southern drawl torturing a scared kid.

The tortured man, held nothing but contempt for the Sheriff. And who could blame him?

"If Buff ever comes to Sparta by himself, I swear I will kill him!" stated Henry (name withheld) to a former lawman (name also withheld).

It was a hot summer night in June, around midnight. The kind of balmy night when all the locusts performed in high-pitched harmony. The sheriff was on his way out the door. Suddenly, Sherrie, the evening dispatcher received a call. It was about vandalism at the Campbell Ford dealership.

"I'll take this. You want to go Sherrie?"

"I'll go, Sheriff!"

The two hopped into Buff's 1978 Mercury Sedan and responded to the call. On the way, a car appeared from nowhere, running a stop sign and forcing the sheriff's car off the road.

Buff swerved, but crashed into a utility pole in a Ramey's store parking lot. Lamb and Tennis were injured, but able to radio for help.

When the ambulance arrived, they took the two to Cox Hospital in Springfield. Sherrie Tennis received several cuts and bruises but was released. Fifty-seven-year-old Buff Lamb received internal injuries and a [125]fractured arm. They admitted him to the hospital.

When asked what happened, [126]Buff stated: "I don't even feel

---

an end in those days.

[125] This writer was told by an ex-wife that they found Buff at the crash scene with his arm bent behind his neck.

[126] Buff went to court over the accident because insurance refused to cover his doctor's bills.

like talking about it!"

The next morning, with Buff in the hospital, a deputy responded to the vandalism call, only to learn that no one from the dealership had called the sheriff's office, nor was there any vandalism to their property.

The call had been a ruse to draw the sheriff out alone. Since his election, Buff Lamb's truck had been stolen and burned. Someone had shot at his head and barely missed, and an unknown assassin had threatened to kill him. Finally, he had been run off the road at least twice. Someone wanted Buff Lamb in the ground.

The most amazing thing is if Buff was being targeted, he told no one about it. He called the near-death accidents, no "big deal".

If people were trying to kill him, they weren't doing a very good job. As for the call about vandalism, Buff alleged it was an assassination attempt. He had received information that two men from St. Louis had called in the ruse.

"The men were waiting in ambush to kill me. If I hadn't been run off the road, Sherrie and I would have been murdered!" If that were true, and there was doubt that it was, Buff knew something no one else did.

Had Buff been caught with some man's wife? Had he bullied the wrong person? Were criminals targeting him for costing them thousands of dollars? No one knew for sure. Not even those he held closest to him.

Most lawmen at this point would have taken a long vacation or armed themselves to the hilt, but not Buff Lamb. Putting him in the ground would mean death to anyone who tried it.

If there was an assassin out there waiting to send a bullet his way, he'd better not miss, because if he did, and Buff got off a shot, hell would claim another soul.

Buff and marijuana plants

CHAPTER EIGHTEEN

BUFF & CORRINE

Buff met Alice Corrine Duckworth by happenstance. She was a tall, thin, brunette, and had a smile that lit up the morning's landscape. Her good looks would shame a beauty queen. Corrine worked as a curator for the Ozark Museum. Their first encounter was through a mutual friend.

"I need someone to barbecue chickens at the Fourth of July celebration in the park. Do you know of anyone?"

"Try the Sheriff, Corrine! He loves to barbecue, and he's an excellent cook."

"The Sheriff?"

"Yeah, Buff Lamb. He's a nice guy and I'm sure he'll do it!"

A week later, Corrine met with the sheriff and was impressed. Buff was polite, charismatic, and every bit the gentleman.

The two dated for a short time and Buff asked Corrine to marry him. December 30th, 1981, Buff and Corrine Duckworth united in marriage at the Riverdale Baptist Church in Ozark. Corrine had two children from a prior marriage. Buff had told her about his son Randy (Roho) Hursh, but she never knew Penny existed. Buff could be very secretive.

In 1981, Buff also met Dwight McNeil. A former Ozark High School graduate with an associate degree in criminal justice administration. [127]Through fishing trips together, Buff became impressed with the young man.

"Dwight, I need a good man like you to take my place when I retire in a few years. You have a lot of good ideas and Christian County needs someone like you!"

"I appreciate that, Buff, but. . ."

"Now, just wait a minute. I haven't finished. If you come on board as my Chief Deputy, when I retire I'll back you in the next election and you'd be sure to win!"

It was an offer too good to pass up for a young man finding his way in the world. Sheriff of the whole County? Dwight accepted Buff's offer.

"Come and see me in my office and we'll try to get this thing moving."

"Thanks, Buff. I mean that."

By the end of 1981, the sheriff's office consisted of Deputies Dwight McNeil, his Chief Deputy, Dale Reynolds, Lyle Hodges, Frank Gray, and Joan Matthews. Dispatchers were Buff's wife Corrine, Lana Sackett, Lyle Rickman, and Danny Clinton. The bookkeeper was Delores Knittle.

Six months after her marriage to Buff, Corrine was busy in her house with her young daughter. It was dark outside. Corrine looked out the window. Two men she had never seen before were sitting in a car in front of the house.

"It was unusually dark outside, and I thought it was strange they didn't get out of the car and come up to the house. After a few minutes, the passenger cracked his door open and I could see the men were armed with rifles. Something was wrong, and a chill ran down my spine. What if the men were there to kill Buff? Or even the kids and me? I grabbed the phone and dialed the sheriff's office for Buff."

"This is Corrine. I need you to send Buff home! Now! There are two men outside the house, and they are armed!"

"He's on the way, Corrine...Buff said to try to get a license plate number if you can."

"I flipped the lights off in the house and got the kids to lie down on the floor. Then I slipped around the back of the house and

---

[127] Springfield Leader & Press December 22, 1982

approached the front from a corner. I quickly scribbled down some numbers and then snuck back into the house. The men must have figured Buff wasn't home because when I got back to the front room, they were gone."

When Buff arrived, Corrine told him what had happened. Buff asked a few questions but didn't seem too concerned. "He was just that way," said the former Mrs. Lamb.

Had the men come to Buff's house to kill him? Were they men Buff had hired? Were they husbands of women Buff had assaulted or stepped out with? Or were they there for Corrine?

Thirty-four years later and Corrine still doesn't know who the men were or why they were sitting outside her house armed with rifles. What happened next may shed some light on that night.

[128]Glenn Spencer of [129]Nixa, who Buff had arrested for selling stolen tractors, was out on a $75,000 bond. Instead of keeping a low profile and putting together a court defense, Spencer met with Jerry Walker and James Huff, at their used car dealership in Hollister, Missouri.

"Howdy boys!"

"Hi, Glenn."

"Have you thought about my offer?"

"You know we thought about that Glenn and..."

"Stop right there! I offered you boys $350 to find me someone, to do away with Lamb permanently, and you boys had better deliver! *I am not messing around here!* I want that sheriff *gone* and the sooner the *better*! And while you're at it, I want Jimmy's arms broken! You boys had better not screw me on this deal! *Now get this done*! The next time I come back here, you had *better* have me a name!"

Former preacher Spencer stomped off the lot as Walker and Huff stood looking at each other.

"What are we going to do Jerry?"

"I don't know, but he's *serious!* He wants that sheriff *dead!*"

"Do you think he might come after us?"

"I don't know, but I think we need to call someone about this."

The two men contacted Deputy Dwight McNeil back in

---

[128] St. Louis Post-*Dispatch* August 17, 1982

[129] The actual city withheld.

Christian County. McNeil, in turn, contacted Highway Patrolman Tom Martin. Along with Sheriff Buff Lamb, and the Christian County Prosecutor, Tim McCormick, the lawmen met with one informant.

The interview was recorded and given to the Taney County Prosecutor, Jim Justus. After hearing the informant's story, Justus immediately filed charges and had Spencer arrested. It appeared as if Deputy McNeil had saved Buff's life.

Meanwhile, Chief Deputy Dwight McNeil was busy making a name for himself. The sheriff had promised McNeil he would not run for sheriff. Buff was almost 60 and his body was feeling the effects of an eventful life. It was time for him and Corrine to retire and enjoy life without the stress of being the county's protector.

There was just one problem, Corrine admitted enjoyed being the wife of the sheriff. And Buff liked the notoriety. Maybe he should serve one more term?

Dwight worked tirelessly for Buff and the citizens of Christian County. McNeil instituted a Neighborhood Watch program, and confiscated over five tons of marijuana in just one summer!

Chief Deputy McNeil took photography classes and set up a photo lab in the jail. The sheriff's department could finally process their own photos. He was an extraordinarily bright and educated deputy.

By July 1983, Chief Deputy Dwight McNeil was all over the Christian County newspapers—just like Buff had once been.

Buff smoked and drank a little. He had also gained a few extra pounds over the years. And he sometimes felt the stress of having lived an extraordinary lifestyle. He wasn't the same man he was ten years ago.

So, it was no shock to anyone when the Lion of the Ozarks suffered a mild heart attack and was hospitalized in Springfield. Buff was no longer the muscled-up, overly aggressive lion he had once been. He was sixty years old, and all the years of pushing his body to the limit were catching up with him.

Buff's doctor gave him some advice: "Buff, you need to slow down, retire, go fishing. Relax, enjoy life. If you don't, this job is going to kill you."

Corrine remembered when Buff was resting at home after the heart attack and received a call from the dispatcher.

"Corrine! Get me my gun. I'm going out on a call!"
"Oh no, you're not! The doctor said you need bed rest!"
"Hell! Then, how about I let you drive?"
"I dunno..."
"Either you drive or I'm going by myself!"

"I'll get my coat." There was no point arguing with Buff once his mind was closed. Corrine had learned that. Buff and Corrine went on the call, and many more after that, all with Corrine at the wheel, until he got better.

The Christmas of 1983 came and went with Buff working to catch burglars and cattle rustlers. Things never slowed down in the hills of Christian County.

But Buff had a secret he had been keeping from everyone but Corrine. A secret he was about to spring on Ozark and his chief deputy, Dwight McNeil.

Buff and Corrine Lamb 1981
(Courtesy Corrine Duckworth).

CHAPTER NINETEEN

I'LL WIN ONE WAY OR THE OTHER

January 1984: It was cold, 32 degrees as the two men stood outside talking. Earlier, Deputy Dwight McNeil had received a call to meet Buff at a secluded location in the county.

When Buff first met Dwight, he convinced him to come on board as his deputy, with the promise that after his term in office, he'd back Dwight for Sheriff. Dwight accepted and over the next few years worked hard for Buff.

In the book "Murder on a Lonely Road" by George Pawlaczyk and Beth Hundsdorfer, Dwight met with the Buff one evening. He took precautions by wearing a wire to record their conversation. He must have suspected something was up.

Buff heard that the Missouri Sheriff's Association had voted in a retirement fund. If Buff would stay in office for another four years, he would be eligible for the sheriff's retirement.

At that meeting, Buff [130]allegedly told Dwight he had changed his mind and would run for sheriff. The two argued and Buff gave Dwight an ultimatum.

He could tell people he was getting out of the race and keep his job as deputy, or he could find a new line of work. The deputy

---

[130] Buff's wife does not recall that meeting ever taking place.

declined Buff's offer and turned in what little equipment he had.

"You know this ain't right, Buff!"

"It doesn't matter. I've decided I'm to be Sheriff again, and there ain't anything you can do about it!"

"You know I'll fight you!"

"I'm not worried about you, Dwight. I'm going to be Sheriff one more time."

The die had been cast. Buff had gone back on his word to retire. There was nothing more to be said. Buff had created a breach between the two former friends.

Soon afterward, Buff spoke to Dwight again, "Dwight, I'm going into the hospital, and I don't want anyone to know it. I may be there for a while and I'd appreciate it if you'd keep it a secret. Just run the office as I would."

"Sure."

Buff filed for Sheriff as promised, and the next day, he entered a hospital and underwent triple bypass surgery. His chances of surviving the surgery were not good. At his age and after the tortures he had put his body through, it would take all he could muster to open his eyes again. A few people prepared themselves for the worst news.

Buff's health was failing him. He was sick and knocking on the creator's door, but his mind was made up, if he survived the surgery, he would spend his last years doing what he loved the most, being the Sheriff of Christian County, Missouri.

Rumors spread about the bad blood between Buff and Dwight. Worse yet, people had discovered Buff's whereabouts. Someone leaked the news that Buff was weak and in the hospital. If anyone wanted the Sheriff dead, he was most vulnerable lying in a hospital bed. Buff's life was in danger. Corrine feared for her husband's safety.

Buff had his share of enemies, some of whom were invariably lurking in the shadows. Buff was an easy target flat on his back in a hospital bed. He needed protection, and he needed it quick!

"I spoke to Buff and hired three friends to watch over him while he was recovering in the hospital. I thought someone might try to get rid of him!" said former wife Corrine.

The surgeons cracked open Buff's chest and operated on his heart. The surgery was a complete success. Once again, Buff had proven himself to be invincible. The aging lawman left the hospital in February and announced he would run for Sheriff again.

Running against him would be Dwight McNeil, Jack Savage, and Bill Ramsey. A week after his open-heart surgery, Buff was lying on the living room couch. The phone rang. There was a disturbance. A weapon was involved. Nowadays, thirty cops would respond to a call like that. But not in small towns in the 1980's. One sheriff, one deputy, or one city cop faced and the bad guys alone making arrests. Most of the time without backup.

"Help me up and get my gun, Corrine! I have to answer a call!"

"No, you're not! You're too sick! You can get one of your deputies to take that call!"

"I'm going, Corrine, and either you can drive me, or I'll drive myself!"

There was no changing Buff's mind. They had been through this before. Buff's stubbornness was like a steel trap. Once Buff made up his mind, you might as well go with it.

Corrine grabbed the keys, helped her husband into the car and took her seat behind the wheel of the patrol car. When the couple arrived at the disturbance, a man was pointing a shotgun at a woman.

"I don't like this, Buff, let's call for help." pleaded Corrine.

"Stay in the car, I'll take care of this!"

"I saw Buff step out of the car and walk up to the man. The man turned toward Buff and pointed the double-barreled shotgun at his chest. I thought for sure Buff was going to die! Buff looked at the man and put his fingers in the shotgun's barrel and pushed it away from him."

"Put this down, son," said the big lawman. "And just like that, the man lowered his gun and Buff sent him away."

As the two headed back to Ozark, Corrine looked over at Buff and smiled. She had married one of the bravest men she had ever known. At any moment, that man could have blown Buff to pieces, leaving her a widow. But her husband, Buff Lamb, was no ordinary man. He was the lion of the Ozarks.

Buff was back in the courthouse. He would not let a simple triple bypass heart surgery keep him down for more than a few weeks. Besides, he had not been happy with the way Dwight had run the Sheriff's office during his absence.

By now, everyone knew Buff would run for sheriff, but what happened next shocked the entire town. Buff publicly fired his running mate and chief deputy Dwight McNeil on February 10th.

The news made the front page of the local newspaper. In a statement to the press, Sheriff Lamb stated he had fired Dwight because of his "job performance". But everyone knew the real reason. Buff fired Dwight because Deputy McNeil was a threat to him winning the election.

A former Green Beret, Nixa Fire Chief, and Buff's Deputy, Jack Savage, put his name in the hat for Sheriff, as did Democrat Bill Ramsey. Bill had been a deputy and the Chief of Police of Ozark from 1979 to 1981. Both men were qualified for the office, but everyone knew the election would come down to Buff and Dwight.

Was it over-confidence, arrogance, his health, or deep down, did Buff know it was time to retire? No one knows for sure why, but Sheriff Lamb campaigned less during this election than he ever had before.

He appeared to the public as a boxer past his prime. He had gained some weight and was much older. The house of his glory days was behind him, and he didn't live there anymore. To be remembered, he needed to leave office while still the champ. To go out on his own terms. Not because of an up-and-coming deputy.

Around this time, Corrine entered the hospital for a common surgery. Because of the bad blood between some people close to him, Buff called upon a few friends to watch over his wife. Maybe they were paranoid, or maybe their concern was justified. Either way, they weren't taking any chances.

There were some legitimate concerns on Buff's part that someone might try to harm Corrine. Not because of her own deeds, but because of his. By now, Buff had a lot of enemies, and harming the sheriff's wife would sure get Buff's attention.

Going back to Buff's and Corrine's concern for their safety

while working at a hospital's ICU unit, Corrine had stepped outside to find that all four of her tires had been slashed. Corrine believed someone did it to send her a message. A warning that she was not welcome there if she was married to the Christian County Sheriff. Buff and his wife Corrine's life was in danger.

In June of that year, papers reported that someone was [131]knocking over Dwight's posters. The sheriff's office said they would prosecute anyone caught in the vandalism, but no one expected the sheriff to catch the culprit. Not when he was the prime suspect!

Back on the home front, even though Buff had a woman who adored him, he could not curtail his cheating ways. One afternoon Corrine received a phone call from a neighbor. Buff had been spending time with another woman. A woman who was Corrine's friend.

When Corrine heard the news, it crushed her heart. How could a man she loved so deeply, disrespect her by spending time with another woman? Until this time in their marriage, Corrine had felt like she was the luckiest woman in the world to have found Buff. And yet, with one phone call, that tower of love and respect came crumbling down. Corrine trusted Buff. His past meant nothing to her.

If Buff was cheating, and she was just now discovering it, other people knew about it. Soon, the whole town would know it and Corrine would fall in line with the rest of the wives Buff had betrayed.

What was she going to do? What if her two kids found out? They loved Buff, and he loved them like his own. They were a family. How could he do such a thing?

Corrine had too much pride to play the dumb wife sharing her husband with the town women. Corrine was no one's doormat and she would not be walked on by anyone. Not even the man of her dreams.

---

[131] A former Lamb friend stated it was common practice to take down your opponent's re-elect signs.

Corrine, described as "beautiful" by Buff's friends, could not abide cheating. Other than the neighbors say--so, Corrine had absolute proof that Buff was cheating on her. It was time to let go of the man who she later called the "love of her life". The couple divorced in April 1984. Buff was sixty years old. The marriage had lasted less than three years.

Buff could see his future slowly collapsing in front of him. His home life was in the commode as well as his political career. He had to do something quickly. His life with Corrine was unfixable. But could he save his job?

Six days before the general election, Buff gathered a plethora of reporters together. He had an announcement. His former deputy and running mate, Dwight McNeil, had misappropriated county funds.

When Dwight heard the announcement he-was-infuriated! How dare Buff make such an outrageous accusation! Who did he think he was? How low was this old man willing to go? Was it worth adulterating yourself just to keep a sheriff's job?

If Dwight did such a thing, why was Buff 'just now' bringing it to light? Buff's election was in trouble, and he had to make voters think Dwight was dishonest. Dwight quickly set the record straight!

In August 1984, Dwight McNeil won the Republican primary. But the sheriff wasn't through yet. A Republican all his life, Buff backed Bill Ramsey, a Democrat for sheriff.

Next, Buff claimed that Bill Ramsey was more qualified for the job. To prove his point, he took out a full-page addition in the newspaper stating Bill's qualifications. [132]Buff committed political suicide to back a Democrat. Just to keep Dwight from winning the election.

In the add, Buff further stated that Ramsey had eight years of law enforcement experience. Compared to Dwight McNeil's thirty-two months. He stated that Bill Ramsey was not controlled by special interest groups, and that his friend Bill had not been fired

---

[132] Buff's frame of mind comes into question at this point. He had set out on a mission to destroy Dwight McNeil's reputation. At all costs!

from a police job as Dwight had been.

The ploy reeked of vindictiveness and revenge. The maneuver would cost Buff more than a few friends and his self-respect. No one liked a sore loser.

When the ballots were counted, former deputy Dwight McNeil won the election. Dwight McNeil had captured the nomination for sheriff. Buff had come to a political end in Christian County. The living legend was fading.

Democrat Bill Ramsey, even with Buff's help, had lost by 183 votes. Proving that Buff Lamb still had influence in Christian County. And that Dwight McNeil was not the superstar that some people had thought.

CHAPTER TWENTY

LAST RUN FOR SHERIFF

Amidst average temperatures of 75 degrees, Ozark threw a retirement party for Buff. Over 300 friends attended. Well-wishers enjoyed barbecued pork, chicken, and beef.

The Ozark Jubilee Band from Branson played in the background. It was a prodigious send-off for the man who had given so much of himself to Christian County.

"What's your plans for retirement, Buff?" Asked Roma Evans. "Roma, I plan to do a lot of fishing and hunting!"

Tony Evans and his wife, Roma, had supported Buff throughout his career. When Tony Jr. had a run-in with the law, Buff treated him fairly. He even tried to take him under his wing to straighten him out. The family loved Buff, and he had been there when they needed him the most.

Charles Gentile and his wife owned a Chiropractic Clinic in Ozark. They had known Buff since 1963 when they were neighbors. Charles even became a reserve deputy and taught CPR to the sheriff's office. The family supported Buff as "their Sheriff" and as a close friend.

Contrary to what the McNeil camp thought of Buff Lamb, many people loved him. Buff loved to barbecue and spend time with friends.

During the retirement ceremony, Buff was presented with a jacket and a plaque for his 30 years of service. It took a lot to soften the lawman, but the kindness of so many friends overwhelmed the legend with emotions. The accolades and gifts were more than Buff had ever expected.

People loved Buff Lamb. He was a Christian County icon and a hero to some. No one could take that away, and few would ever achieve it.

Along the way he made enemies, but every sheriff does. It is impossible to make everyone happy at the same time. Someone is always going to feel like they got the short end of the stick.

The problem was that law enforcement had changed, but Buff had not. Now it was McNeil's turn for retribution. Sheriff Dwight McNeil filed a libel lawsuit against Buff in November 1984.

The suit claimed three million dollars in damages to the former deputy. Rather than take it to court, Buff's bonding agent agreed to pay McNeil an undisclosed amount to settle. Buff's power was gone. His wings had been clipped. He was grounded. Buff could no longer soar like an eagle. All he had left were a few faithful friends and his memories.

Dwight McNeil's first year was fraught with tough cases. There was the unsolved murder of a woman named Jackie Johns, and dead bodies had shown up in Christian County.

After one year in office, McNeil stated: "It has aged me. I feel like I'm 100."

And there was the [133]Delmina Woods Camp. The sheriff and his deputies had been receiving complaints about the camp for a long time.

[134]During the early morning hours of April 24, 1986, Dwight and his deputies loaded into pickups armed with pistols and shotguns and headed to the youth camp. Dwight had decided to close the juvenile camp after a recent 16-year-old escaped the facility. There had been a series of runaways, but nothing was being done about it.

Jefferson City Officials at the state capitol pledged they would move the camp elsewhere, but that could take a year and cost

---

[133] A State Facility for Juvenile Offenders.
[134] Springfield Leader and Press May 4, 1986 page 19.

Missouri over a million dollars. Something had to be done, so Dwight took action.

When they arrived, the kids and staff were at breakfast. Dwight and his deputies [135] arrested fifteen staff members and took twenty-eight juveniles into custody.

Staffers were taken to jail, and the boys and girls were taken to a Youth Services office in Springfield. It looked like the problem had been solved. But it was just beginning.

On May 5th, 1986, the Missouri Attorney General stated that he would not file charges against Dwight and his deputies for closing the camp. But that the camp "would be re-opened" and that such actions by the sheriff's office would not be tolerated.

[136] Dwight had found disfavor from the highest law enforcement entity in the state. All the charges against the Delmina staff were dropped. But it didn't end there.

Several of the Camp employees sued the Sheriff, causing more stress to an already over-worked, underpaid, and totally vexed administration.

Camp employee Ronnie Lewis asked for $485,000 in compensatory damages and one million in punitive damages. Years later, one plaintiff allegedly received $90,000 from Dwight's bonding company.

The raid on the camp would continue to haunt Sheriff McNeil for the rest of his career. Early in January, Dwight made an announcement. "I have a rare opportunity in another field, and I will not be running for sheriff." Translated: He was getting out of the law enforcement business.

When Buff heard the news he immediately announced his candidacy for Sheriff. Even though he had supported a Democrat in the last election, he felt like he had a good chance of winning.

"I encouraged Buff to run," said former wife Corrine Duckworth.

The former lawman was feeling good about his prospects in the upcoming election until July 1988. That's when the Springfield News-Leader carried the front-page headline: "Seized items

---

[135] Ann Carter wrote an editorial in the Springfield Leader and Press dated May 4, 1986.

[136] He was and still is a Hero to some over his decision to close Delmina Woods.

unaccounted for under Buff Lamb's tenure."

The article accused [137]Buff of not returning confiscated items to their rightful owners. Guns, money, and jewelry had come up missing in the sheriff's office during his tenures.

When Buff left office on December 31st, 1984, he took everything! The comparison inventory showed that he had taken $5,375 worth of county equipment.

Buff fired back. He refused to comment on the subject unless charges were filed against him. But he would cooperate by taking a polygraph test. He later changed his mind.

"I am not going to get involved with anything unless somebody wants to charge me!" The article by Bill Maurer came at an inopportune time for Buff.

As the vote for county sheriff continued, Buff saw himself losing the election. The front-page article had swayed voters against him. Just as the unsolved murder of Carol Blades had back in 1969. Even today (2017) there are people in Ozark who believe Buff had something to do with Carol Blades' murder.

Republican Steve Whitney won the 1988 GOP primary and election. Once again, the county had spoken: The aging lawman, now almost sixty-five, was out of date. Much like the timeworn western lawmen of the 19th century. It was time to give up the hope of ever wearing a badge again. That day comes for every lawman.

Buff Lamb's methods of justice had been effective in the 1940s, 50s, 60s, and 70s. But the county and state were changing, just like the basic principles of law enforcement.

Buff had reigned courageously and bravely, but those days had passed. And it was now time to write another chapter in the life of Buff Lamb.

Dwight McNeil, who did not run in 1988, ran a successful Private Investigation business. Dwight ran for Christian County sheriff again in 2000 but lost in the primary.

Fifteen years later, by a twist of fate, Dwight would find himself back in the Ozark Courthouse.

---

[137] In Buff's defense, this writer met an attorney who recalled going to a Lamb auction. He stated he remembered it clearly.

In 2015, Dwight McNeil was asked to take over as interim sheriff. Sheriff Joey Kyle had resigned in 2015 after pleading guilty to embezzling county funds.

For a time, Buff fell into a deep pit of depression. In 1989, at age 65 Buff's health was deteriorating. He had regrets about not spending time with his daughter, Penny.

His past haunted him and he questioned his decisions. Buff remembered his six ex-wives and the life he had with them. Jean E Ray, Ruby Jo, Mary Lee, Luella, Clara, and Corrine. All of them had been special in their own way.

At least one person stated, "Buff was not in his right mind. I worried about him. He'd fade in and out."

Buff had divorced and then tried to reconcile with Corrine, but her mind was made up. She'd never go back to Buff. Corrine remembered the day she received a call from Buff to come over to his house.

"I need to see you, Corrine."

"Buff I..."

"No, I need to see you! Can you come over?"

"Okay, I'll be there as soon as I can."

When Corrine arrived, Buff didn't look like himself. He was pale and withdrawn. The two sat at Buff's dining room table and spoke for a while talking about old times.

Buff tried to convince Corrine to come back to him, but it was useless. He was a broken man. Corrine felt sorry for Buff, but there was nothing she could do.

"You know you can't date or re-marry and keep my name?"

"What do you mean?"

"You *will not* date or see anyone as long as you have my name!"

"Okay." Corrine began to be frightened.

Then Buff said and did something that would haunt Corrine for the rest of her life. Something so bizarre and scary that she told no one except her daughter and family.

"I think it's time you learned your lesson."

Corrine's former husband reached over and loaded a revolver with one bullet. He spun the cylinder. Without hesitation or speech, he pointed the gun at Corrine. She was maybe two feet away from him. Corrine began to cry and plead with Buff.

"Don't do this Buff! I have children! Please don't do this!"

Buff pulled the trigger. Click! The hammer dropped, but the gun never fired.

As calmly as he had picked it up, Buff set the revolver back down. There was a deafening silence in the room. Corrine froze and her world stopped turning. What had just happened? Was this real? After a few moments, Corrine quickly rose to her feet and exited the house. She was in shock. Her mind was numb.

Buff had finally hit rock bottom. In a moment of weakness and despair, he had attempted to kill someone he had once loved. Buff had clearly lost his mind, if only temporarily.

By all odds, Corrine should have died that day, but the Angels were watching over her. That day, that hour, would live with her for the rest of her life.

In the years that followed, Corrine saw and spoke to Buff one more time. The gun was not brought up. Her marriage, friendship, and attraction to the man she once loved were over. She didn't know Buff anymore. He was a different man.

Had the gun fired, Corrine would have been dead and Buff in all likeliness, would have turned the gun on himself.

The years came and went for Buff with bouts of depression and sickness. There were also the dreams that haunted him from the life he had once lived.

He was sometimes lonely and spent as much time as he could with his family back in Kentucky. Then a miracle happened.

In 1989, the husband of Arlene Mae Davis passed away after thirty-eight years of marriage. Arlene, who owned the Hilltop Drive Inn in Ozark had 3 sons: Ken, Larry, and Jeff.

In 1990, Arlene dated Buff, whom she had known for many years. The two married in 1991. Buff was Arlene's second husband. Arlene made [138]Buff's 8th time standing at the altar.

Arlene made Buff the happiest man he had ever been. Arlene was a good woman, and she cared for Buff. Everyone around them could see how much they adored one another. Buff's hound dog days were over. He had found the love of his life and he would never stray from home again.

Buff and Arlene enjoyed retirement. The two had a travel trailer

---

[138] I have been told Buff was married over 8 times but could never confirm it.

and often went camping with friends. Buff was an avid outdoorsman.

Buff and Arlene led a quiet life on a rented farm just outside of Ozark. Buff survived off a tiny pension and disability for his crippled legs.

At one point, an infection had developed in one of his legs and the doctor wanted to amputate it.

"You are not taking my leg, Doc! I'll live with the pain if I have to, but I'm keeping the leg!" The leg remained.

In his retirement years, Buff could have spent time in coffee shops and cafes, regaling locals with his exploits as one of Missouri's most famous lawmen. But he didn't.

In the late 1980s, a film producer approached Buff about making a movie about his life. In 1973, the film Walking Tall had premiered in drive-ins across the nation. It was allegedly the true story of the life of Sheriff Buford Hayes Pusser in Tennessee. The movie was a hit across America but there has been some doubt about its historical accuracies since then.

Somehow, someone in Hollywood had heard about Buff and his exploits. The movie would be about a cowboy turned daredevil, turned marshal, turned sheriff. About a man who had carried and wielded a five-cell flashlight on unruly lawbreakers. About the legend who had rallied a town together to stave off a motorcycle gang. About the man who had been challenged and stood up to bullies and marijuana growers. There was enough there for a movie and a whole lot more.

"They want to make a movie about my life, [139]Jeff."

"You should do it, Buff!"

"Naw, no one wants to hear about me" and Buff got up from the table and walked back into the kitchen to help Arlene.

When interviewed in 2017, Stan Shelton, a former Reserve Deputy, stated that he was at Buff's house and saw a check and contract regarding making a movie about Buff's life. But nothing came of the movie. Maybe Buff just wasn't interested.

Buff chose a quiet life. He cut wood on his farm, watched western movies, and spent time with his family and friends.

Buff's stepson Ken Davis, claimed, "Even as a 70-year-old

---

[139] Jeff Richards

man, smoking cigarettes, Buff could out-work a man in his twenties. Buff was a man who I never saw get upset or lose his temper," Buff's stepson Ken Davis.

By 1999, Buff was no longer a threat to anyone and was often seen sitting in a wheelchair. The life he had led had taken its toll. He was an old man and struggled to keep a smile and handshake for his friends. His last public appearance came when he rode in a car during a parade in Ozark. It was the last time his friend Gary Heatherly would see him alive.

After several strokes, the Sheriff who had become a legend in his own time passed away. It was on a Friday, November 16th, 2001 at Cox South Hospital in Springfield, Missouri.

"His heart just gave out", said Buff's nephew, Dennis Beckett.

Before he [140] passed, Buff had been ill, and he and Arlene had survived on their modest earnings. Several of Buff's friends chipped in to help Arlene buy a tombstone for her beloved husband.

Louard Elbert (Buffalo\Buff) Lamb's passing signaled the end of an old-time City Marshal and Sheriff. The days of protecting your town from bikers, drug dealers, and thieves were gone.

Buff Lamb protected his county with his reputation and his determination to uphold the law according to his interpretation of right and wrong. It was a tough job that called for a tough man. Was Christian County a safer place to live when Buff Lamb wore a badge? YOU BET IT WAS!

---

[140] Buff's nephew, Dennis Beckett never heard of Buff's children Penny or Roho until the funeral. Dennis had spent the summer of 1969 with Buff and Clara and Buff had never mentioned his kids.

Buff's birthday party. Buff sitting with cowboy hat on.

Buff Lamb
— a name about every one knew.
I met Buff when he first come to Christian county, I think in the early 40's. Come here with Ravens Circus & Rodeo Co. He was one of the best friends I could ever had. I enjoyed lots of Fishing & Hunting Trips with him. I also had 16 yrs as a special Deputy Sheriff under Buff. I've been with Buff in tuff spots that I know would a been alot worse if he had not been there. I have so many good memory I wouldn't take anything for. Buff was a man that would give the shirt off his back. a good friend a good person and good lawman. I know Buff will always be missed.

a friend forever
Everett Ball

ABOUT THE AUTHOR

Randy H. Greer has cultivated a lengthy career in law enforcement. After serving four years in the Army, Greer became a police officer before moving on to the field of corrections, where he worked in the Missouri State Penitentiary, eventually retiring from the Federal Bureau of Prisons. Since retiring, Greer has worked as a bailiff and a licensed private investigator with the State of Missouri.

Greer has coupled his personal experiences with his passion for history and investigative writing resulting in two prior publications, *Echoes of Mercy*, stories from behind the walls of the Federal Medical Center Prison, and *King's Corners*, a collection of Greer's experiences as a small-town police officer.

In this book, Greer profiles one of the last "old time" sheriffs, Buff Lamb. Lamb's controversial means of meting justice, his ongoing romantic entanglements, and his larger-than-life persona often left the citizens of Christian County reeling. Greer has spent the last several years researching newspaper archives, following up on rumors, and interviewing friends, family, and co-workers of the late Buff Lamb to reveal the truths and tales surrounding The Lion of the Ozarks.

People Interviewed for this Book

Clady Beckett: Louard Elbert "Buff" Lamb's only sister.
Dennis Beckett: Buff's Nephew. Dennis spent summers with Buff.
Penny Glossip: Buff Lamb's daughter.
Clara Anderson: One of Buff's ex-wives 1968-1980.
Corrine Duckworth: One of Buff's ex-wives 1981-1984.
Shannon Duckworth: Stepson of Buff Lamb.
Ken Davis: Lamb stepson.
Lyle Hodges: Former Lamb Deputy.
Russell Heatherly: Former Lamb Deputy.
Wandal Heatherly: Former Lamb Deputy.
Gary Heatherly: Former Lamb Deputy.
Dale Reynolds: Former Lamb Deputy.
Joe Asher: Former Lamb Deputy.
Danny Clinton: Former Lamb Deputy.
Anonymous: Former Webster County Deputy.
Bob Scrivener: Former Lamb Deputy 1976-1978.
Clara Clinton: Wife of former Lamb Deputy Gale Clinton. Clara knew Buff's wife Louella and Mary Lee Blevins.
Ray Speak: Former Ozark Police Chief.
Paul Weeks: Former Lamb Deputy 1977-1978.
Kent C. Casey: Former Missouri Highway Patrolman and friend of Lamb.
Marcelene Casey: Wife of former Lamb Deputy Ben Casey. Knew Buff and his wife Louella very well.
Nancy Young: Wife of former Reserve Deputy Kenneth Young.
Frankie Danderson: Brother of Reserve Deputy Orville Danderson.
Anonymous: Springfield, Missouri Police Officer.
Pletcher Rogers: Former Rockaway and Ozark, Police.
Paul Blue: Paul was Buff & Carter's friend in the 1940's.
Evelyn Gentile: Friend of Buff Lamb from 1963.
Wilma Cantrell: Lamb friend 1940s-1980s.
Roma Evans: Friend of Lamb.
Knial Iorg: Rode in patrol car with Buff as a teenager.
Jim Kirkland: Met Buff Lamb.
Donald Kisse: Rode with Buff in his patrol car as a teenager.

J. Patrick Sullivan: Attorney.
James Mitchell: Reserve Deputy for Sheriff Mickey Owen.
Carolyn Savage: Husband was Buff's Chief Deputy 1977-1978.
Rob Savage: Nephew of Jack Savage.
Charlotte Hall: Daughter of Wandal Heatherly and Lamb friend.
Gerald Shelton: Remembered Joe Patton incident.
Jamie Newman: Remembered Buff Lamb.
Dennis Hanks: Remembered Marshal Lamb in 1963.
Colette Long: Met Sheriff Lamb. She was a waitress at the time.
Larry Barnts: In a car stopped by Buff.
Kenneth Johnson: Attorney for Lamb ex-wife.
Kathy Monger: Jack Monger's daughter in-law.
Charlie Hedin: Buff worked for Charlie's dad as a laborer.
Kathy Jackson: Remembered Buff 1968 or 1970.
Jeff Richards: Knew Buff in his later years.
Douglas C. Snyder: Met Buff Lamb.
Jim Moody: Met Buff Lamb.
Greg Stumpff: Knew Buff Lamb as a kid.
Becky Pyland Davis: Knew Sheriff Lamb.
Kirk Smith: Knew Sheriff Lamb.
Stan Shelton: Friend of Buff Lamb.
Janet Heatherly: Knew Buff Lamb.
Bill Ramsey: Knew Buff. Once shot and killed a man with a shotgun in self-defense.
Joe Asher: Former full-time deputy.
Kim Owen: Information on Bud Holman.
Dwight McNeil: Former Lamb full-time deputy & sheriff.

SOURCES

"When Isam was Sheriff" by Susie Knust.
"Springfield News-Leader"
"Springfield Leader and Press"
"Facebook Blogs"
"Ancestry.com"
"Newspapers.com"
"Christian County Republican Newspaper"
"Nixa Enterprise Newspaper"
"Greene County Public Library"
"Christian County Public Library"
"Christian County Museum"
"Christian County Courthouse (old)"
"A Body on a Farm" by Barbara Kemm-Highton
"Murder on A Lonely Road" by George Pawlaczyk and Beth Hundsdorfer
"Wayne Glenn's Christian County History A-Z"
"Somewhere in Time 170 Years of Missouri Corrections" by Mark Schreiber and Burkhardt Moeller.
"Official Program: Christian County Centennial 1859-1959"
"Buford Pusser The Other Story" By Mike Elam

www.ingramcontent.com/pod-product-compliance
Lightning Source LLC
Chambersburg PA
CBHW071952070426
42453CB00012BA/2137